# Minsky

Key Contemporary Thinkers Series includes:

# Minsky

Daniel H. Neilson

polity

First published in 2019 by Polity Press

Polity Press
65 Bridge Street
Cambridge CB2 1UR, UK

Polity Press
101 Station Landing
Suite 300
Medford, MA 02155, USA

ISBN-13: 978-1-5095-2849-3
ISBN-13: 978-1-5095-2850-9 (pb)

A catalogue record for this book is available from the British Library.

Typeset in 10.5 on 12pt Palatino
by Fakenham Prepress Solutions, Fakenham, Norfolk NR21 8NL
Printed and bound in the UK by TJ International Limited

The publisher has used its best endeavours to ensure that the URLs for external websites referred to in this book are correct and active at the time of going to press. However, the publisher has no responsibility for the websites and can make no guarantee that a site will remain live or that the content is or will remain appropriate.

Every effort has been made to trace all copyright holders, but if any have been overlooked the publisher will be pleased to include any necessary credits in any subsequent reprint or edition.

For further information on Polity, visit our website: politybooks.com

# Contents

*To my parents*

# Acknowledgments

I am deeply appreciative of the support of Diana DePardo-Minsky, Alan Minsky, and Esther Minsky in producing this book. My debts to Perry Mehrling, beyond the many citations in the pages that follow, cannot be listed exhaustively. I will mention only two: thank you for showing me Minsky, and thank you for teaching me how to be an economist (though I do it differently than you!). I have been enjoying conversations on all subjects with Tyler Bickford, Çağlar Girit, and Jackson Jones for decades now, and perhaps they will find some of those ideas reflected in these pages. Chris Coggins has been an inspiring co-teacher and friend. I thank Asma Abbas, who among many other lessons pointed me to Rancière (1987), where I found Jacotot (1823), which has been indispensable. An anonymous conversant helped me learn to navigate with map and compass. Whitney Harris was a dedicated research assistant and an indulgent counterparty in conversation and study. I am grateful to my students, and in particular to Jacques Ben-Avie, Mario Campbell, Mackenzie Dwyer, Darcy Pollard, Alice Sinclair, Jeff Tsen, John Zhang, and Chandler Zincke-Byer, each of whom taught me something during this project – thank you, it is what sustains me as a teacher.

I am grateful for and humbled by the work of three anonymous reviewers who read a quite rough version of the manuscript. I responded to many if not most of their suggestions in the text, sometimes by clarification rather than a change in course. I am likewise grateful for the editorial interventions of George Owers and Fiona Sewell at various stages of the process. The book is undoubtedly improved by all of these contributions, though I take responsibility for what remains.

Lena and Augie, I am inspired by how you love your work, and from you I am learning to love my own. Sara, you are present in every word, in every chapter, and in the entire book, but still I feel I have only just begun to speak to you.

# 1

# *Introduction*

## Theory, history, discipline

In writing this text, I have sought to reconcile my commitment to two sometimes conflicting aims. On the one hand, it is meant to be a concise outline of Minsky's work, consistent with the aims of Polity's *Key Contemporary Thinkers* series, in which this book appears. Indeed, there is an interesting challenge to the task of somehow representing in a single text the entire work of a scholar; nor will I object if whatever attention might come to the book comes first and foremost in search of an understanding of who Hyman Minsky was.

On the other hand, in celebrating and exploring the work of a single person, it is easy to fall into the trap of hagiography – to make the erroneous leap from "Minsky said it" to "it is true." Minsky said many things, to many different audiences, that responded to the events and debates of his time, many of which are already fading into history. If one's only aim is to know what Minsky said, one might therefore simply re-read his many publications, as I have done in the preparation of this book. One finds there a lively and synthetic thinker who has perceived something important and who tries many avenues to get it across.

With this book I have sought, instead, to create something that adds to Minsky's intellectual bequest. In sorting through that wealth, I have accepted the assessment of my teacher Perry Mehrling that the value of Minsky's contribution lies not in any particular investigation, but in "his way of looking at the world, his underlying vision" (Mehrling 1999, 139). I have also followed this recommendation of Minsky's:

> The main issue in the controversy about what Keynes really meant is not the discovery of the true meaning of the "Master's" text. The main issue is how to construct a theory that enables us to understand the behavior of a capitalist economy. (1978d, 6f.; also 1990c)

As Minsky approached Keynes, so I approach Minsky. I share the goal of understanding capitalism, and in particular the role and status of finance in that system. I share with Mehrling and many other observers the belief that Minsky offered us a valuable vision through which to do so. In taking on the events and debates of his time – in academic writing, in commentary, and in engagements with his fellow economists – he put that vision to use, and in the process left us a legacy: the trace of an underlying, never fully spelled out theory. That theory, as I will show, though it is certainly present in Minsky's published work, does not stand perfectly well on its own in its original form.

This book is not history of thought, nor is it biography. It is a concise outline of Minsky's thought, but that outline is the consequence of my own synthesis and consolidation. I have tried everywhere to represent Minsky's intention unambiguously, but at the same time I have avoided supposing that what Minsky said is, by that fact, necessarily true. Rather I have assumed that Minsky's work may be valuable in the worthwhile but incomplete task of understanding capitalism; I have tried to convey something of that value, and to suggest what use might be made of Minsky's work by another generation of students of society.

In doing so, I have developed three main threads over the course of the book. The first thread is financial theory. Minsky offered a theory of how financial capitalism works, which has the virtue of also giving insight into how it fails. He perceived, in my view, enduring patterns of the financial system and of market society, and it has been my goal to organize these – in a way that Minsky never did but with which I think he would agree – into a theory of capitalist finance. This is done in the main text of chapters 2, 3, 5, and 6, and is what I would consider to be the main contribution of the book.

Dealing with Minsky's theoretical contributions has required, to some extent, a factoring out of financial history, the story of the crises that motivated Minsky and provided him with an ongoing source of inspiration, examples, and evidence. Minsky's own writing is less accessible, some decades on, for its being tied to circumstances that have changed. One begins to resent ninety-five pages on the crisis of 1975 in *Stabilizing an Unstable Economy*! The reader who wishes to catch up on the history of the financial crises of the latter half of the last century is directed to Wolfson (1986), for his systematic presentation of each of the relevant episodes; what discussion I have included here of this history is largely confined to brief illustrations that are relatively self-contained and do not presume much in the way of prior knowledge.

At the same time I have felt it important to say a bit about the global financial crisis of 2008. This comes, first, in the form of a narrative in the last section of this chapter. Second, I have made extensive use of the report of the Financial Crisis Inquiry Commission (FCIC), created by the US legislature to investigate the causes of the crisis. The report is based on extensive interviews, and so in many cases it allows a direct view into the motivations and perceptions of those actually involved in how the events played out. I have taken from that study numerous illustrations of what Minsky understood to be parts of the general pattern of financial crisis. For a more analytical look at the 2008 crisis I recommend the characteristically efficient and insightful analysis of Mehrling (2010).

Minsky offers not only a theory but also a way of being an economist, which is the subject of the second thread of this book. In sections set in differentiated type, this thread proceeds in parallel with the first. Unlike the theoretical development, which is organized to present the theory coherently, this thread is organized chronologically. It considers, in order, Minsky's major works (his dissertation, two books, a major research study, an edited volume, and an important series of papers), and in doing so illustrates how Minsky came to know what he knew. This second thread ends with a consideration of contemporary interpretations of Minsky.

The third and final thread takes up the relationship between Minsky's work and the economics literature. Minsky was a stern critic of many of the main currents of economic and financial theory. He objected to the assumptions that underlie the IS–LM model, in Minsky's time a major framework for economic analysis and still the main teaching model in undergraduate macroeconomics. Minsky felt that IS–LM lacked a role for realistic financial relationships, which were for him the driving force in an understanding of economic activity. Neither was this critique directed only toward

IS–LM: at many turns, Minsky's focus on finance was the basis for divergence from existing theory.

As a consequence of these objections, Minsky worked at the margins of the economics profession, a topic that runs through his writing from the beginning right to the end. He addressed his colleagues with engagement, despite his frustrations with the trends in assumptions and methodologies of economics that came and went during his time. Rather than rejecting economics entirely, he took refuge among others on the margins. He found allies and an audience there, but they were not spared his criticism either. I have tried to make a constructive contribution without rehashing well-known debates about what is wrong with economics. Minsky, I argue, was trying to express something that is very difficult to express in the language of economics, and this is so for interesting reasons. In chapter 4, I try to be precise about the points of divergence, those specific aspects of Minsky's financial capitalism that are incompatible with economic theory and practice. I come back to this in chapter 7, where I ask what work has come out of this incompatibility.

In the next section, I introduce the themes of the book in a skeletal form. The section that follows illustrates the disciplinary context in which Minsky worked, for those who might be unfamiliar with economics. The final section of this chapter is a brief reading of the global financial crisis of 2008.

## Time, uncertainty, capitalism

Hyman P. Minsky (September 23, 1919–October 24, 1996) began his career as an economist with the completion of his doctoral dissertation at Harvard University in 1954. The experience of the stock market crash of 1929 and the subsequent Great Depression led Minsky, like many of his profession, to the question of whether another large financial disturbance could occur – whether "it" could happen again. Unlike most of his colleagues, he felt compelled to study at first hand the detailed workings of the financial system, the infrastructure of capitalism. This took the form of a study early in his career of the Federal Funds market from a seat in a New York money-market broker, and from 1967 as a consultant to Mark Twain Bank (1957a; Mehrling 1999).[1] Minsky concluded that not only

---

[1] Citations showing a year without author refer to single-authored works by Minsky, e.g. (1954).

could instability recur, but in fact it would necessarily do so, and that such instability was indeed to be expected as a normal part of the functioning of US capitalism.

The crises of the 1960s and 1970s seemed to be powerful evidence in favor of this hypothesis. Much of Minsky's work on the financial system is written in response to the financial disturbances he observed. His narrative evolves in response to these, but to a significant degree it is the same story each time. The crises that attracted Minsky's notice were these: the Kennedy Slide of 1962 (1962; 1963a); the 1966 Credit Crunch (1965c; 1968b; 1968c; 1969a; 1969b); the Penn Central liquidity squeeze of 1969–70 (1970a; 1971; 1974a; 1974e); the international monetary crisis of August 1971 (1972a; 1973a); the Franklin National crisis of 1974–5 (1974d; 1976; 1978a; 1978e; 1986e); the 1978 intervention in the exchange value of the dollar (1978f); the silver crisis of 1980 (1980a; 1981b; 1982a; 1983a); the Continental Illinois crisis of 1984 (1984d); and the 1987 financial crisis (1988a; 1988c; 1988d; 1989b; 1992a; 1993a; 1995b). Crisis did, indeed, seem to be normal.

Minsky drew a stark conclusion from these crises, one that was to define his thinking, his career, and his legacy: "[I]n the early 1960s the mode of behavior of the financial system underwent significant changes and ... these changes tended to accelerate the trend toward fragile finance" (1975b, 10; also 1995a). Following a stable period between the end of the Depression and the mid-1960s, crisis had become, if not predictable, at least unsurprising. These crises were costly, in terms of unemployment and bankruptcies, and instability seemed to be getting worse, so an investigation was warranted; Minsky's first-hand observations in financial institutions suggested that that investigation should begin from the financial mechanics.

The acute nature of crisis – headline-making defaults and institutional failures – points to the importance of *time* in understanding them. Each crisis has a before, in which financial patterns are established and elaborated; a during, when those patterns seem to unravel chaotically and damagingly; and an after, characterized by retrenchment and stability. The cyclicality of crisis, however, seemed also to demonstrate that each post-crisis period becomes, imperceptibly, a pre-crisis period. Minsky saw this temporality embedded in the financial system. "As a result of their debt structure, firms operate today with cash-payment commitments inherited from the past. Furthermore, current investment and ownership of capital assets require financing, which sets up payment commitments for the future" (1982d, 19). Instability, that is, emerges in the present, as promises made in the past are reconciled against an ever-unfolding future.

The unstable present stands between a past that can no longer be changed and a future that cannot yet be fully known. Business ventures into this uncertain future, with entrepreneurs making promises now, to be fulfilled with the eventual proceeds that follow from today's efforts. It is in the financial system that the success of these ventures will ultimately be tested, when debts made today come due in the future. Time and uncertainty create the possibility for innovation, for the setting in motion of business activity on which capitalism is based. They also, Minsky saw, create the possibility for failure; not just for the failure of a single firm, but for widespread failure due to systemic phenomena. Because the financial system is where past and present meet, it is the locus for crisis.

Minsky thus took as his object of study the capitalist system, with the financial system at its center (1967a). Pervasive uncertainty meant that finance, and thus capitalism, would be constantly subjected to the possibility of crisis. The series of crises over the course of Minsky's career seemed to provide clear evidence that the US financial system was indeed unstable, and that that instability even arose out of the normal operation of the system. He went so far as to call financial capitalism "inherently flawed" (1969a, 224): "The flaw in American capitalism centers around the financial system, and the financial system is an essential attribute of the economy" (1968a, 578).

The ramifications of time and uncertainty are written into the financial system; the resulting instability of capitalism constitutes its inherent flaw (1996). The investigation of this problem set Minsky in motion, and sustained his entire career. There seemed to be plenty to talk about, and one might suppose that Minsky's contributions would have found an attentive audience among his fellow economists.

* * *

To know Minsky's economics, we must also know Minsky as economist. Viewed in its entirety, Minsky's published work follows the contexts, events, and debates of his time; he draws on texts, conversations, and experience and incorporates each into a worldview, a theory that is constantly refined, updated to add what is new and subtract what is no longer true or no longer needed. In each of Minsky's publications we can see not only knowledge but also a way of knowing. In learning from Minsky we must study both: not only what he knew but how he knew it. For the events and debates of our time are not those of Minsky's time; his ideas cannot be taken up unaltered. They must be interpreted, given meaning in our own context. Minsky's way of knowing will lead us to our own. Thinking back to his days as a student, the septuagenarian Minsky wrote:

> [T]here is never a true reading of a text. The reader is not a mere passive recipient, but an active creator of interpretation. The reader brings priors to the text, priors that can be more or less restricting or binding. In economics, there is another difficulty: history unfolds and institutions evolve. As the world moves through time, each reader has to interpret (extract meaning from) events and institutional changes and integrate the reading of what happened and what is into an interpretation, into a maintained theory. This means that, to a serious scholar, the lessons learned from a text are subject to change. (1992b, 365)

Minsky's scholarship began with the completion of his doctoral dissertation at Harvard in 1954. His subject was business cycles, a problem of unquestionable importance, in light of the experience of 1929 and the Great Depression that had been the economic context for his formative studies. It seemed also to be a promising line of research: economic theory did not yet offer satisfying answers. Minsky found a disconnected body of thought, with each author emphasizing a particular phenomenon, attached to a different policy approach; what was lacking was an integrated work that transcended these compartments. The Great Depression had demonstrated that a severe crisis was a phenomenon that cut across the fields of economic experience, that needed to be understood from a synthetic point of view. For a PhD student, such an approach would be ambitious, but Minsky had learned to put vision before technique (1992b; Mehrling 1999). If the result would be received as "eclectic," so much the better: the problem had enough texture to warrant it. He begins:

> Paraphrasing Voltaire, we can assert that if business cycles did not exist, the economic theorist would have invented them. For if we look at the problem of business cycles, without any doctrinaire bias, it seems obvious that in this branch of economics a natural connection occurs between the often too separate compartments of economic analysis: between the "monetary" and the so-called real phenomena. Therefore, a theory of business cycles, to be consistent with the observable material and the inherited doctrines, should be a blend of the analytical material which deals with the interrelations among a few broad

aggregates – which traditionally has been the approach of monetary theory – and the analytical material which deals with the behavior of individual economic units and of particular markets – which has been the sphere of price and distribution theory. This thesis can be interpreted as an attempt to construct such an eclectic business cycle theory. ([1954] 2000, 1)

Minsky had lost his dissertation supervisor, the great Joseph Schumpeter, with his death in 1950. Though Minsky completed his project under the supervision of Wassily Leontief, he remained Schumpeter's student, and the dissertation was the beginning of an effort to build on his professor's work. Schumpeter had placed finance at the center of his understanding of economic change. Credit extended in support of business activity is the mechanism by which entrepreneurs are given control over the means of production, even before those efforts bear fruit:

> By credit, entrepreneurs are given access to the social stream of goods before they have acquired a normal claim to it. It temporarily substitutes, as it were, a fiction of this claim for the claim itself. Granting credit in this sense operates as an order upon the economic system to accommodate itself to the purposes of the entrepreneur, as an order on the goods which he needs: it means entrusting him with productive forces. (Schumpeter 1934, 107)

The financial system is not just a way of allocating command of production. As the very organizing principle of capitalism, finance is itself the most important of the evolving institutions to which economists must attend; in the financial record is written the unfolding history of the entrepreneurial successes and failures of capitalism: "Schumpeter brought to the analysis of a monetary production economy the sense of the economy as an evolving institutional structure. Nowhere is market-driven institutional evolution (innovation) more apparent than in the financial sphere" (1993c, 113). But Schumpeter's work on business cycles did not, Minsky thought, fully incorporate the lessons of the Depression. The contradiction was surprising, to a mature Minsky looking back, for Schumpeter had many of the necessary ingredients at his disposal:

> [Schumpeter] noted that "The money market is always, as it were, the headquarters of the capitalist system" (Schumpeter, 1934: 126). This seemingly implies that the sequence of events that can be said to have been triggered by the break in stock market prices in October 1929

– that led to the complete closure of the banking system in March of 1933 – was not peripheral but rather were central to the functioning of a capitalist economy. ... Schumpeter may write of financial catastrophe, but he nowhere explains catastrophe. The significance of liability structures and the importance to banks as holders of business liabilities of business profits are only peripheral concerns in Schumpeter's analysis in *The Theory of Economic Development* and *Business Cycles*. (1986c, 114)

Minsky already had a sense of his vision, his maintained theory; here was a set of historical circumstances in need of interpretation: to explain catastrophe. If the money market, the banking system, is the center of capitalism, why should the financial structures that unraveled in the Depression be relegated to the margins of analysis? It would become the effort that was to form the intellectual basis of his career. "To Schumpeter's original view of the monetary process we have to add a specific consideration of the liquidity phenomenon" ([1954] 2000, 225). To interpret catastrophe would require that liability structures, and the sudden intervention of crisis in the normal functioning of capitalism, be placed at the center.

\* \* \*

## Minsky as economist

Minsky's training – Chicago BS in mathematics (1941), Harvard PhD in economics (1954) – started him off with the makings of a disciplinary insider. After teaching at Brown while still a graduate student, he accepted a faculty position at Berkeley in 1958. His education and early publications in academic journals of high prestige among economists (1957a; 1957b; 1959a; 1961) might have set him on the path to prominence. But he left Berkeley for Washington University in St Louis, and his subsequent publications are in more marginal academic journals and in the non-academic press. Minsky never withdrew his claim on economics, however; instead he resolutely and repeatedly sited himself at its margins.

This must be in part because Minsky's treatment of themes central to his work is in conflict with those of the discipline. The issues of time and uncertainty created serious problems for economists, he thought, and the mechanisms of finance suggested a way to study them. "Economics is a strange discipline in which present, past, and future coexist in time. A cash-flow approach to economic theory helps unravel some of the problems associated with time" (1982d, 19; also 1993b). Minsky's objection echoes that of G. L. S. Shackle: "To look down the complete vista of all relevant history-to-come is to see a still picture where nothing happens. In such a world ... there would be no need for postponement of choice, no need for liquidity" (Shackle 1972, 165). For Shackle as for Minsky, economics offers no adequate understanding of time, and therefore no adequate understanding of instability.

Minsky did try to persuade. His dissertation (1954) can be understood as a way to add financial mechanics to standard economic models. His first book (1975c) adds very much the same financial mechanics to the analysis of Keynes's *The General Theory of Employment, Interest and Money* (1936). Minsky's second book (1986e) studies them in the context of the experience of the 1970s. Indeed, what is most striking about Minsky's relationship to the economics profession is the consistency of his stance despite the changing fashions of academic economics.

In this it seems helpful to regard the economics profession as a community united by a language. Economics has its lexicon of technical terms – or everyday terms with technical meanings – but also a vocabulary of mathematical models and statistical approaches. Together, these comprise the language of instruction in most economics undergraduate and especially PhD programs. Minsky certainly mastered the language to the satisfaction of the Harvard economics department, but later reflection, without regret, suggests that he still felt a language barrier, having "never really [become] strongly bound to [his] contemporaries in economics" (1985b, 213).

The resulting communication difficulties were clearly frustrating. Reviews of work by more mainstream authors open with complaints: "The combination of a critical attitude towards Arrow–Debreu and a positive view of Keynes led this reader to expect that an effort to develop an 'alternative construction' would follow... Alas, my high hopes were not validated" (1984c, 450; also 1981c). The reviews that follow are embedded in what are clearly rehearsals of Minsky's own views; it is not hard to see how these jabs could be ignored by their targets.

Fellow dissidents received much the same treatment: Minsky's review of Davidson's *Money and the Real World* suggests that the author "should go back to the drawing board and produce a more succinct and a better focused presentation of the important things he has to say" (1974b, 17), and the review makes clear that the ideal model for such a presentation would be Minsky's own. Writing of Leijonhufvud's *Information and Coordination*, similarly, Minsky says that it "works to the literature, not to institutions and their evolution. This was valuable when criticising established doctrine was the task; it is a serious flaw when the task is the building of viable theory" (1982e, 977).

Minsky's objections extend to the methodologies that sustain the language of economists. He dismissed as irrelevant to practical concerns highly mathematical theoretical and statistical models: "Economic policy is not made for a mathematical or statistical abstraction" (1977g, 3; also 1969c; 1980d). Statistical analyses were "printouts": "As the doubters of permanent prosperity did not have printouts to prove the validity of their views, it was quite proper to ignore the arguments drawn from theory, history, and institutional analysis" (1977b, 146). Such modeling efforts were not just idle; the standards of mainstream economics meant that other valuable perspectives – principally, again, Minsky's own – were ignored. Evidently the failure to communicate was a sore point; evidently Minsky's tone did little to win converts to his perspective among his colleagues.

This book seeks to understand Minsky's work; the opinions of the mainstream of the economics profession are well documented elsewhere, as are those of its heterodox critics. I have therefore limited myself, in what follows, to the critical aspect of the relationship between Minsky and the economics profession: what are the points on which communication failed, and why? Minsky returned time and again to the same set of ideas about finance and capitalism, trying to articulate them to other economists, but economics did not really have the vocabulary to accommodate those ideas. As Shackle observed, "Money, as something which can introduce a time-interval between selling one thing and deciding what to have in exchange for it, can evidently have no place in a system whose logic requires all its choices to be comprehensively simultaneous in order that they may be pre-reconciled and thus fully informed" (Shackle 1972, 164).

The real barrier to communication, I propose, was that the themes Minsky dealt with – uncertainty, liquidity, money – find no easy expression in the language of economics as it currently is; the very words had different meanings to his colleagues. The more one is socialized into the discipline, the harder it becomes to talk about these ideas. I return to these translation difficulties later, especially in chapters 4 and 7.

\* \* \*

Minsky's intellectual vision and appetite for the grand challenges of the theory of business cycles made Schumpeter a natural mentor. The author of a thousand-page book on business cycles illustrated by example a way of knowing, a way of being a scholar and an economist, that Minsky admired and sought to emulate. But Schumpeter's approach was out of sync with the priorities of the post-World War II generation of graduate students. The ambition that Minsky shared with Schumpeter was the exception among his cohort of PhD students:

> [I]n the Harvard of 1946–49, the graduate students, largely but not exclusively veterans of either the service or of Washington, did not take Schumpeter seriously. This was not because the students were in the forefront of the emerging mathematical economics and therefore had surpassed Schumpeter. It was because the main thrust in economics at Harvard was applied: the simplified Keynesian economics of Prof. Alvin Hansen and the quite mechanical application of monopolistic competition theory to problems of industrial organization as set out by Prof. Edward Mason ruled the roost. The representative student was not intellectually engaged with the big issues of the scope and nature of economics and the lessons for a vision of society that were to be extracted from the dismal history of the previous two decades. The prevailing ethos was careerist. The working postulate among the graduate students was not only that big thinking was in the past, but, in truth, it was not worth doing. Their task was to get the Ph.D. and go forth to teach or to serve a government bureau. In the prevailing view, economics was now a normal science, not a grand adventure, and therefore Schumpeter was irrelevant. (1992b, 363 n. 2)

Minsky had no interest in the mechanical application of theory; he wanted the grand adventure. This meant that he was immediately confronted with the contradictions of economic theory. This led to, for example, challenging the distinction made by economics between monetary phenomena, reckoned in quantities of money, and "real" phenomena, reckoned in quantities of goods, from the first paragraph of his dissertation (the substance of which distinction we will take up again in chapter 4). Schumpeter had also rejected the distinction:

Economic action cannot, at least in capitalist society, be explained without taking account of money, and practically all economic propositions are relative to the *modus operandi* of a given monetary system. In this sense any theory of, say, wages or unemployment or foreign trade or monopoly must be a "monetary" theory, even if the phenomena under study can be defined in non-monetary terms. (Schumpeter 1939, 548)

It was not only in studying money that Minsky felt the need to reject the methodological assumptions of the economics discipline:

Much of present day price theory tends to identify price theory with marginal analysis. Marginal analysis is far from being a primitive concept; it is derived in the analysis of perfect competition. Marginal analysis is derived from profit maximization ... the carrying over of profit maximization behavior to non-competitive markets has been the typical approach as far as price theory is concerned. Economists can be accused of being parrots who say that marginal *x* equals marginal *y*, and the position so determined is where the firm will operate.

Observed behavior of firms, any casual observation of the behavior of certain non-competitive firms during an inflationary period, can be interpreted to indicate that firms either lack the knowledge or the desire to behave as the marginal analysis indicates a firm should behave. The use of unmodified profit maximization as the sole basis for the analysis of firm behavior is a carry-over by the economist from the analysis of competitive markets. ([1954] 2000, 90f.)

Minsky did not hesitate to object to these two weaknesses of economic theory – leaving no room for money, and adherence to marginalism against the evidence: "The usual economic theory ignores financing problems and assumes a unique behavior principle for all firms (profit maximization, leaving only the trivial problem of the choice of the product to be produced to the firm" ([1954] 2000, 89). By relegating finance to the margins, by supposing that money is to be distinguished from what is "real," by assuming a single mode of economic action, economists had assumed away the possibility for crisis. Without an understanding of finance, what could they say about the crash of 1929, or the closure of the banking system in 1933?

\* \* \*

## The crisis of 2008

In writing about financial crisis, a perennial topic and the one that oriented Minsky's career, two points in time inevitably loom large: the next crisis and the last. Knowing that they come about, if not cyclically, at least repeatedly, it is hard to resist the temptation to imagine what will be the next crisis. Minsky's work, as we shall see in some detail, helps us see how financial traumas grow from the quiescent periods that precede them; but having recognized this fact, one can quickly spot the seeds of crisis all around. This is not the same, however, as being able to offer a precise prediction. For these reasons I have tried, in what follows, to avoid predicting the next crisis; we shall have to wait and see.

The last crisis stands out in memory; indeed, a decade on, the debates and headlines that occupy the world's attention today can still be traced along quite short paths back to the events of 2008. The subprime crisis, or the global financial crisis of 2008, was a major disruption: from a tipping point in the market for US real estate, it exposed the fragile arrangements in a global market-based credit system, bringing about the failures of major financial institutions, sparking a crisis in sovereign debt, and requiring coordinated intervention by central banks around the world. The consequences for employment, public finances, investment, not to mention politics and even, arguably, the course of history, have been and continue to be great. At the same time there is a risk of driving in the rear-view mirror, of preparing for the last war. Financial crises have a strong family resemblance, and at the same time each is unique; Minsky's work, I argue, is more about the family resemblance than about any particular crisis, 2008 included.

I have aimed, therefore, to keep 2008 as an important example, but not the focus, for most of the book. Chapter 7 takes up the subprime crisis as a context for understanding the resurgent interest in Minsky's work. Examples from the FCIC of the US Congress are included throughout the book as illustrations, in many cases quite precise ones, of Minsky's insights. This section anticipates the discussion to follow with a short look at the events of the 2008 crisis. (I have tried to make this narrative both complete and efficient; as a consequence I fear it is slightly technical for an introductory section. To the interested reader for whom some of the financial vocabulary may be daunting, I suggest that you feel free to skip or skim this section. Its value might lie mostly in that it summarizes the events of the 2008 crisis from a viewpoint theoretically consistent with the other chapters of this book, and so I also suggest that you come back to it at the end.)

One of the signal developments in the world of finance in the decades leading up to 2008 was a shift from a bank-credit-based to a market-based financial system; borrowing and lending that had been conducted via customer relationships at commercial banks came, more and more, to be conducted instead via the exchange of securities. The year 2008 can be understood as the first major crisis of this new, market-based financial system. These developments in banking were driven in particular by the rise of money-market mutual funds (1980e). Money funds emerged beginning in the late 1960s, and their usage grew as a response to the demand for high interest rates as compensation for rising price levels in the high-inflation years that followed. They sought to provide the benefits of bank deposits – stable value and ready convertibility into cash – while paying an interest rate above the Depression-era Regulation Q caps, upper limits on interest rates set by the Federal Reserve, that bound commercial banks. They operated as mutual funds, issuing shares and using the proceeds to purchase securities. Though money funds were not insured, as commercial bank deposits were by the Federal Deposit Insurance Corporation (FDIC), they succeeded in displacing the bank credit that had dominated.

As depositors' business moved from commercial banks to money funds, borrowers' business moved from commercial loans to commercial paper – short-term securities issued by companies to finance their immediate cash needs. Issuers were able to place their commercial paper with money-market funds, which in their turn needed securities to hold. Bank-based credit was thus displaced by market-based credit; the normal banking transaction was now the issuance of commercial paper matched by the issuance of money-market fund shares, rather than the creation of a bank loan matched by an increase in deposits.

Viewed in the abstract, the two approaches to finance, bank-based and market-based, are not so different. In practice, however, they interacted differently with the institutional environment. One important set of institutional developments was around regulation – indeed the very fact that money funds were not bound by interest-rate ceilings was the main factor behind their growth. Another relevant regulatory shift was the 1999 repeal of the 1932 Glass–Steagall Act, which had kept commercial banks out of securities-based banking. The expansion of market-based credit went along with a general decline in the regulation of the financial system; financial markets were left to their own devices.

A second set of institutional changes relates to the financial usages that supported securities-based banking. One of the institutional advantages of market-based credit over bank loans was that securities could readily trade in secondary markets: the initial purchaser of newly issued commercial paper was not obligated to hold it to maturity, as was the case for bank loans, largely unmarketable. Such markets were made by securities dealers, who bought and sold such securities. The existence of these markets seemed an unmitigated good: knowing that the position could readily be liquidated, potential lenders would enter the market more willingly, and borrowers would benefit from more competitive rates and smoother issuance. Securities dealers thus became more central to the flows of credit; their business was in turn supported by the growth in repurchase agreement (repo) markets. A sale-and-repurchase agreement is a short-term loan of cash, secured by a financial asset: the owner of the asset can post it, overnight or for a very short term, as collateral for a loan of cash. The repo market facilitated the short-term holdings needed by securities dealers.

As money-market funds seemed to improve on bank deposits, the market-based credit system seemed to improve on the bank-based system, and it grew accordingly. An innovation that would prove critical in 2008 was securitization: a group of financial assets was pooled, the cash flows generated by them assigned according to a structured issuance of securities. It is market-based banking taken to its logical conclusion – a purely financial entity that fit easily into the infrastructure and usages of market-based finance. There was much to argue in favor: as Minsky had said (two decades earlier), it "makes the steps in financing explicit. It allows separate organizations to carry out the steps that were previously folded into banks and other financial intermediaries. Securitization will obviously impose a dynamics to financing that may well lead to a greater decentralization and variety of forms of financing than now exists" (1990b, 65).

In a way, this is just banking: instead of a commercial bank funding a portfolio of loans with deposits, it is an investment vehicle funding a portfolio of bonds with securities. One innovation that seemed even to improve upon institution-based banking was that a single securitization vehicle could issue a range of liabilities with different levels of debt seniority. This was the most alchemical of achievements of the market-based credit system, for it meant that a set of even doubtful assets could be the basis for the issuance of high-quality, money-like securities, perfect for the portfolios of money-market investors seeking an alternative to cash. The most junior tranches of securitizations could even serve as the basis for a second-order securitization, thus the collateralized debt obligation (CDO).

Securitization reached its high-water mark in the US real-estate market; the steady origination of mortgages was a supply that could meet the steady demand for mortgage-backed securities. The availability of such wholesale funding supported the issuance of large amounts of new mortgage financing, which in turn supported a steady rise in home prices. The appreciation of real-estate prices meant that borrowers could readily sell into a rising market in the event of payment difficulties. As a result the increased lending seemed sustainable, and moreover seemed to support the wholesale financial innovations underlying the expansion of retail lending. In the final phase of the housing boom, demand for mortgage securitizations was great enough to impel a relaxation of lending standards: confident that any level of issuance would be absorbed, mortgage originators sought to lend to anyone and everyone, even those "subprime" borrowers with little or dubious credit history.

A final innovation that accompanied and enabled the rise in securitized finance was the use of credit-default swaps (CDS), which can be understood as insurance policies on market-based credit instruments. A CDS contract is written between a buyer and a seller, with reference to a security issued by a third party. The buyer of CDS pays the seller a periodic premium; in the event of default by the issuer, the seller of CDS pays the buyer a principal. It functions as insurance against default, but because one can take a position in CDS with no interest in the underlying security, such swaps also provided an inexpensive vehicle for speculation. CDS can be written against any security; CDS on mortgage-backed securities played an important role in the expansion of market-based credit before the crisis of 2008.

Elements of the market-based credit system had been tested, in particular during the 1970 crisis in the commercial paper markets, and the 1982 crisis in the repo market, but in retrospect these were little more than bumps in the road. Repo, commercial paper, securitization, and credit-default swap markets grew significantly over the subsequent decades, and became closely connected to the boom in residential construction and mortgage finance. In general, despite the anxieties of some, the US financial system seemed, in the early 2000s, more stable than at any time in the past, and the peaks and troughs of recessions had lessened, dubbed the "Great Moderation."

The crisis unfolded in stages from early 2007 to its apex in September 2008. In the early stages of the crisis, payment problems associated with some of the most adventurous mortgages – the subprime segment of the market – began to emerge, casting doubts over the US real-estate market more broadly. Concerns simmered about the housing market, about the extent of market-based credit that had been extended on the basis of housing loans, and about the potential of losses in these markets to affect major financial institutions. Disruptions in funding markets were evident but the extent of the crisis was not yet widely known. Broadly speaking, owners of mortgage-backed securities were beginning to seek an exit from these positions, and securities dealers, as the proximate intermediaries supporting such business, accommodated this exit by purchasing the securities from those who wished to sell. The dislocation was evident in short-term interest rates, in particular in the cost of repo borrowing against Treasury collateral, which became very cheap relative to borrowing against mortgage-backed security collateral. Borrowing was still possible, but anxiety about financial stability was becoming widespread.

The Federal Reserve (the Fed) did not offer major interventions in the early stages of the crisis. In March 2008, however, the hastily arranged acquisition of investment bank Bear Stearns by its erstwhile competitor JPMorgan Chase marked a shift to a more acute period, and the central bank increased its efforts to support the financial system. Recognizing that the rise of securities-based finance meant that securities dealers were the key intermediary, evident in spiking borrowing costs and increasing dealer reliance on short-term borrowing, the Fed aimed to support a general exit from mortgage-related assets by easing dealer financing conditions. It offered a range of special credit facilities to shore up dealer finance directly or indirectly through dealers' banks. Notably, the Fed deployed its own, pre-existing reserve of Treasury securities to fund these interventions, without expanding its balance sheet from its pre-crisis size of just under $1 trillion.

These interventions calmed markets for a time, but September 2008 brought a new wave of failures, bringing the crisis to its peak. The government-sponsored enterprises Fannie Mae and Freddie Mac, instrumental in providing mortgage finance in the US, were placed in receivership on September 7; investment bank

Lehman Brothers, heavily exposed to mortgage-backed and other securitized credit, declared bankruptcy on September 15; and insurance company American International Group (AIG), with extensive CDS business, declared bankruptcy the following day. Other institutions, large and small, in the US and internationally, seemed to be in jeopardy. Financial markets came to a halt. The Fed responded with a much more direct presence in the market-based credit system. It rapidly expanded its support to banks and dealers, expanding its balance sheet by $1.4 trillion by December 2008 (with a further $2 trillion to come by January 2015). The special liquidity programs were unwound over the course of 2009, as the central bank settled eventually on the absorption of much of the US mortgage market onto its own balance sheet. By expanding dealer finance, and then acting as a dealer itself, the Fed absorbed major parts of the global money markets onto its own balance sheet; it purchased a huge swath of the market-based credit system (Grad, Mehrling, and Neilson 2011; Mehrling 2010).

The interventions did resolve the acute phase of the crisis, though the wider repercussions were still severe. It is difficult to bracket the endpoint of the crisis – in the US, it led to a major recession. The pre-crisis unemployment rate was not seen again until 2017; the pre-crisis employment-to-population ratio remains distant as of this writing (2018). In Europe, the US events contributed to an extended crisis in sovereign debt, in turn shaking the foundations of the eurozone and the European Union. The contraction and financial disruptions were felt around the world. The populist and proto-fascist political movements that have come to prominence in 2008's wake surely owe some of their rise to resentments stemming from the crisis and its aftermath.

The crisis prompted wide reflection on the excesses of the boom, on the appropriate scale of the financial system, and on the sustainability of capitalism itself; these reflections continue as 2008 is interpreted in light of what has followed. As a consequence, the work of Hyman Minsky, who argued that "stability is desta-bilizing," has been seen as relevant once again: his books were republished, and a range of interpretations have been advanced. This book is more about Minsky's work than it is about 2008, but my own education, and so my interpretation of Minsky, have been strongly shaped by the events described in this section. I shall return to Minsky's role in current debates toward the end of the book; for now I turn to the main event.

# 2

# *Financial capitalism*

## The institutions

Minsky's renown is unquestionably due to his contributions to the understanding of financial stability, but his intellectual ambition was to understand not only finance but capitalism itself. Finance figures not as a kind of business done by a certain class of institutions, but as the very logic of the entire capitalist system. This logic, Minsky saw, operates at the most basic level of economic activity, even those market transactions that appear far from the provinces of finance *per se*. A system based on such logic, he argued, would tend repeatedly toward crisis, and events over the course of his career seemed to bear him out. Financial capitalism and its cyclical patterns are the subject of this chapter and the next.

Financial capitalism begins from the idea that every decision-making unit – business, household, or government – faces the same problem as that faced by a bank. "Banking is a pervasive phenomenon, not something to be dealt with merely by legislation directed at what we call banks" (Simons 1948, 172; Minsky 1977c). Banking, for Minsky as for his teacher at Chicago, Henry C. Simons, is not an activity limited to the institutions that go by that name. In this section this idea is developed in the context of Minsky's early work on poverty. His insight into the financial logic that underpins all of market exchange distinguishes Minsky's approach to the issue of inequality; the insights it yielded confirmed for him the merit of the financial perspective.

If banking is not something done only by banks, then what is it? "[A]ll units are like banks, i.e. a bank has to stand ready to pay cash as deposits are withdrawn; an ordinary firm or household has to be prepared to pay cash due to its liabilities even though its available cash receipts vary" (1972c, 208; also 1962; 1964a; 1972d; Ferri and Minsky 1992). The main problem that a bank faces is to be able to pay back its depositors on demand – a bank that cannot do so is quickly out of business. Though the immediacy of their obligations to depositors makes the problem most acute for banks, it is a problem faced by every actor – the need to pay debts as they come due. This simple abstraction – units facing a cash-flow problem – is ever-present in Minsky's financial capitalism.

The more overtly financial implications of the idea that "everyone is a bank" will take up much of what is to follow. But Minsky used this financial lens as a way into not-overtly-financial questions as well; it shows up in work on poverty, labor markets, and aggregate demand early in Minsky's career, from the mid- to late-1960s, around the declaration of the so-called War on Poverty under US President Lyndon Johnson. Minsky took up the question of poverty as essentially one of banking, where the source of cash was wages, at least for those who were employed.

In this view, the problem of poverty is that wages may be insufficient to provide households with the cash flows consistent with an acceptable standard of living. There are two versions of this problem. For those poor who have jobs, the problem is that their wages are not enough. There is cash coming in, but it is not enough to pay the cash commitments of everyday life in market society. As a consequence, Minsky argued, those in poverty who have jobs are unfairly being made to pay a subsidy to those making more; that subsidy comes in the low price of their services. This imbalance is of sufficient social moment to justify government intervention in the labor market, but what intervention? Simply expanding government spending on public works would not effectively reduce poverty for those workers, because public-works spending would reach a different, comparatively affluent, segment of the labor force (1965a). Shifts in the structure of aggregate demand would instead be needed, to direct spending toward those whose wages most needed to be raised.

For those in poverty who did not have jobs, the problem was different: outside of the labor force as they were, simply expanding demand – whether from public or private sources of spending – would be unlikely to provide any additional cash inflow to such households. They could be reached by transfer schemes, or by intervention in the structure of the labor market itself, to bring the unemployed into work. Minsky objected, however, to the work-training programs for the unemployed created by the War on Poverty legislation, which he saw as an undemocratic – and ineffective – attempt to change people rather than improving the system (1965e). He celebrated instead the programs of the New Deal (1933–6), which "took workers as they were and generated jobs for them. The resurrection of WPA [Works Progress Administration] and its allied projects should be a major weapon in our war on poverty" (1965a, 12; also 1983d). The economic system – US financial capitalism – was not providing an adequate standard of living for all, and it was the system that needed to change, not the people.

The point was to ease the financial, cash-flow constraint that characterized poverty. But the minimum wage, Minsky argued, is ineffective by itself for this purpose – there are large excluded groups, most particularly those without work. Instead, the entire income distribution could be affected by using policy to create a tight labor market – one in which jobs were plentiful, and in which wages would thereby be bid up, as employers sought to fill open positions. This would ease poverty for those with jobs and create jobs for those without (1968a; 1986d). The ideal centerpiece of such an effort would be to use public funds to hire anyone who wished to work, at a minimum wage that would rise steadily over time. This standing labor bid – the employer of last resort – would make the minimum wage *effective*: it would not apply only to those who had jobs already. Anyone who wanted to work could earn at least that wage. This would also allow intervention to make the income distribution more egalitarian over time, by raising the standing labor bid wage more quickly than the average wage (1959c; 1965a; 1966c). Poverty, for Minsky, is a financial problem; it is the insufficiency of cash inflows to cover cash commitments. The solution is to use a public source of funds to improve the distribution, and reduce the uncertainty, of those inflows; it combines egalitarian aims with a technocratic will to intervene in the structure of the system.

After a series of papers addressing the War on Poverty, Minsky mostly turned his attention to matters where the financial perspective was more obviously applicable, and the audience more receptive. Questions of labor and poverty moved into the background, but his way of thinking about them held fast. Writing two decades later, he interprets "the cost of corporate bureaucracy as a financial (payment) commitment" (1984e, 97), drily commenting that, although the employment of blue-collar workers, like intermediate inputs, can be reduced quickly in the face of low sales, corporate bureaucracy is able to protect itself. Middle management, that is, creates wage commitments that must be financed or paid with cash; it is a burden no less crushing than debt (1984e).

His early engagements with questions of poverty were important ones for Minsky. His departure from Berkeley in 1965 appears to have been a choice to put academic work before political activism (Mehrling 1999). Writing from his new position at Washington University in St Louis, Minsky reflects: "Early in the preparations for a possible war on poverty, I was drawn into discussions dealing with the prospective campaign. My view was summarized in the subtitle of a talk at the Berkeley conference, a subtitle that was too flip for the editor of the published version. The subtitle was 'Is This Trip Necessary?'" (1968d, 328).

The intervening years had included the Crunch of 1966, the first serious financial crisis of Minsky's career as an economist. The crisis challenged his thinking about poverty; it meant that the benefits of stability and growth had to be weighed against the costs of the subsequent crisis. Policies that contributed to the boom had to be evaluated for their contributions to the bust. Still, that crisis strongly confirmed the idea that "everyone is a bank," matching cash inflows with maturing cash commitments. The core of Minsky's financial capitalism was settled, and he would never see reason to deviate from it.

The term "financial capitalism," which I have chosen to use here to describe a market pattern based on payment, certainly echoes the label "finance capitalism" due to the German economist and social theorist Rudolf Hilferding (1981). Hilferding's concern, along with that of many who have followed, was to understand the shift from the prominence of industry to the prominence of finance as the most apparent surface of capitalism. The salience of finance signals a new set of social patterns, and a new high-water mark for the reach of the market into all social spheres. Minsky's situating of the logic of finance at the most basic of market transactions, I think, reveals a continuity underlying this break, one that could inform more recent critical studies taking up the social status of finance (Jameson 1997). Minsky himself, however, did not engage along these lines, and so I leave them aside in the present work. I return to related questions that go under the heading of "financialization" in chapter 8.

* * *

Minsky the graduate student sought to cast off the artificial restrictions of economic methodology; placing vision ahead of technique, he was set to understand the potential of capitalism for crisis and instability. From Simons and Schumpeter he had learned to study the monetary system; from his dissertation work he had begun to understand the financial origins of systemic fluctuations. The summer of 1960 brought an opportunity: a study for the Commission on Money and Credit (published in 1964). It was an ambitious and wide-ranging effort by the young Berkeley professor to assemble the pieces of a new type of economic analysis, one which would put money and banking at the center so as to directly address the problem of instability and crisis. Six years earlier, Minsky had objected in his dissertation to the compartmentalized business cycle analyses that were then current. The 1960 study sounds the same call with greater confidence:

> Economic analysis lacks an over-all, integrated view of the financial system of a private enterprise economy. There are separate analyses of the various parts such as financial intermediaries, the monetary system, corporation finance, government finance, and private finance. But there is no over-all view of the financial structure and relations and how these aspects of a private enterprise economy affect its functioning: whether functioning is measured on the "micro" level of the efficient allocation of resources and the distribution of income or on the "macro" level of employment, stability, growth and price level behavior. (1964a, 184)

Minsky laid out not only what the study would do, but how it would do it. The underlying premise, the analytical starting point, as in the dissertation, was to put financial concerns properly at the theoretical center, and to build a comprehensive macroeconomic model. The scale of the study, and the availability of data through the Commission on Money and Credit, created the opportunity to demonstrate that this novel and expansive vision, against the grain of the economics profession, could yield some insight into the problem of financial instability. Minsky recognized that to carry this out, he would have some convincing to do: "However, since this paper 'sells' a point of view – that financial relations are important in determining the stability characteristics of a private enterprise economy – it is necessary to sketch an approach to the study of financial systems" (1964a, 184). Much of the point of the study, that is, was to argue for the analytical approach; the unfamiliarity of such analysis would require patient explaining.

The theoretical portions of the 1960 study make this case for an expansive understanding of the position of finance in capitalism, encompassing not only commitments that are explicitly associated with financial entities, but payment commitments of all types. Minsky wanted to show that instability could arise as the financial structure changed over time, and to do this he needed a notion of finance that was more general than any specific financial usage or instrument. Finance had to be abstracted, that is, from its specific institutional forms, so that the consequences of payment commitments could be seen: "The legal aspects of the contracts are not of primary relevance for our purposes: what is of major importance is the way in which the contracts result in a division or partitioning of the risk and uncertainty inherent in any economic activity" (1964a, 185). The result is a broad concept of the balance sheet, a statement of an actor's assets and liabilities. It is of a kind with the accountant's balance sheet, but conforming to Minsky's goal of communicating the financial structure rather than to an accountant's goal of communicating the financial position of a single entity. The balance sheet becomes a theoretical tool:

> A concept of the balance sheet that is more general than the normal presentation and which would be desirable from our point of view is one in which all contractual payment commitments of the type that a unit cannot default on without penalty are entered as liabilities and assets: lease contracts are liabilities and assets as much as mortgages, etc. This would give us a more accurate picture of the financial commitment of a unit especially for periods when firms are trying to conserve their cash or minimize their debt–equity ratios. In the argument that follows, the propositions that are stated are true for this expanded type of "balance sheet." (1964a, 231)

The balance sheet, that is, is the basic unit of the financial structure; each actor's balance sheet constitutes a node, a point in the financial network, with assets and liabilities constituting edges, links between the nodes. Over time, these links are realized as payment commitments are fulfilled as agreed or, sometimes, are defaulted on. The balance sheet became a pivot point between the theoretical side of the study, which looked at patterns of financial behavior, and the empirical portion of the study, which attempted to measure the financial structure directly.

* * *

## Evolving financial structures

The balancing of cash in- and outflows constitutes the most basic problem faced by all actors in a market system. To understand how they balance such flows, and the consequences for systemic change of this transactional starting point, Minsky envisioned a financial structure: the collection of all payment commitments among all actors. Systematic changes in the pattern of payment commitments can be understood as changes in the financial structure. To see how individual actions contribute to this aggregate evolution requires the notion of a portfolio decision.

As their struggle to meet cash commitments with the proceeds of their cash inflows can be understood as a problem of banking, actors' choice of what payment commitments to make and to accept can be understood as a problem of portfolio choice. This is Minsky's interpretation of capitalism's premise of private ownership. His concept of ownership, however, is not just about the means of production – it is more financial, and more encompassing. Minsky focuses instead on abstract wealth, on the existence of private net worths. If people can own things, if they can own assets, in particular financial assets, then they must decide what to own. And if they can borrow, if they can issue financial liabilities, then they must decide how to borrow, and when and from whom. They must make these portfolio decisions, moreover, in the presence of funda-mental uncertainty. "The essence of capitalism is that units have to take positions in an uncertain world" (1980e, 515; also 1967a).

Each economic unit's portfolio is described, at any moment in time, by its balance sheet, which records what is owned and what is owed. The balance sheet is one of the basic statements of business accounting, but from the beginning, Minsky used it to describe all economic units, whether bank or business or household ([1954] 2000, 89). The balance sheet records assets (what is owned) and liabilities (what is owed); assets entitle the owner to future cash inflows, liabilities commit the issuer to future cash outflows. In this understanding of ownership, the most generic entry is the loan: a promise of cash from borrower to lender. A productive asset is not much different: its owner holds it in anticipation of deriving future flows from it.

From this point of view, a labor contract can be thought of as a financial arrangement – a flow of future wage payments. The wages a worker anticipates receiving are essentially an asset, a stream of future wage inflows. Likewise, the wages an employer anticipates paying are essentially a liability, a commitment to future wage payments. A productive asset, a factory or machine, for example, also can be thought of as financial: it requires a commitment to operation, maintenance, and upkeep; it yields a potential flow of income payments to its owner. In Minsky's financial capitalism, all such arrangements can be generalized to be balance-sheet entries.

What to own and what to owe becomes a portfolio decision. As the problem of meeting cash commitments with cash receipts provided a financial abstraction for that daily need, the problem of selecting a portfolio provided Minsky with a financial abstraction at a more structural level. He saw these financial ideas as a productive and relevant way to address problems arising from the tendencies of financial capitalism, unlike the abstractions of his colleagues, which take little notice of payments and portfolios. It is "the economics of this, a capitalist, economy. It is unlike neo-classical economics which is the economics of an abstract economy" (1972c, 208).

Portfolios, the totality of assets and liabilities, constitute society's financial structure. They reflect decisions made in the past about what positions to hold; they also constrain future behavior (1962). But the unfolding of time is a constant source of novelty, and so actors' opinions about their portfolios are in constant flux. There can be a gap between the portfolios that actors actually hold, and what they might like to hold, and so there is constant impetus to adjust portfolios.

During a boom, to take a particularly important example, apparently attractive opportunities abound, and actors wish to take advantage of them by expanding the speculative assets in their portfolios. There can never be enough money to chase them all. In such circumstances, Minsky observed, those who command a surplus – the owners of private net worths – look for new ways to make use of what funds they have. Thus one of the characteristics of a boom is the appearance of new ways of borrowing and lending. Entrepreneurs, bankers, and speculators push for expansion, allowing a portfolio shift into the booming assets. Regulators and legislators, attentive to the possibilities for excess, push for restraint, limiting these financial innovations (1964b; 1974c).

Just so in the run-up to the 2008 crisis. The Glass–Steagall Act of 1932 had separated the activities of commercial banks and investment banks: the former could not participate in securities markets, the latter could not take deposits. Speaking in 1999, just as the separation was being undone, then Fed Chairman Alan Greenspan argued that this partitioning, a constraint on the use of private net worths, was a source of stability – with business in legislatively isolated markets, investment and commercial banks would be less likely to face difficulties at the same time, and so could support each other in times of distress – a "spare tire" for the financial system (FCIC 2011, 56; also Minsky 1995c). By 1999, however, the memory of 1929 was seven decades distant, and opportunities were more plentiful than money. In the heady years of the dotcom boom of the late 1990s, these arguments outweighed the concerns that had underpinned support for Glass–Steagall. The Gramm–Leach–Bliley Act of 1999 reversed the separation of commercial and investment banks: "The strategies of the largest commercial banks and their holding companies came to more closely resemble the strategies of investment banks. ... Both prospered from the late 1990s until the outbreak of the financial crisis in 2007" (FCIC 2011, 56). The tight money of a financial boom drives changes in the patterns of financial usages.

The cyclical character of this push-and-pull can already be seen: when opportunities seem to outweigh money, private actors seek to make what they have go further, and new financial patterns and instruments are created. Those charged with systemic responsibility – governments, regulators, central banks – push for restraint. The arrangement is not symmetric; the owners of private net worths are rarely seen clamoring for restrictions on how they can allocate their funds. During a period of tight money, a boom, the financial system is thus pushed to evolve in such a way as to make more money available for speculative opportunities (1957a). Such financial innovations increase the number of claims on each dollar of private net worth; in doing so, the possibilities for loss increase. This is precisely the intent of the innovations – though the arguments made in their favor discount the likelihood that those losses will ever materialize.

Another financial innovation that featured in the 2008 crisis put new institutional clothing on old banking bones: shadow banking. In 2008, shadow banking centered on securitization – financial products created to make liquid secondary markets for otherwise illiquid loans, especially mortgages. But thirty years prior, Minsky had written about "fringe" banking, emphasizing its peripheral position relative to the commercial banks: "business lending by finance companies and the issuance of commercial paper by corporations, REITS [real-estate investment trusts], and nonmember commercial banks" (1975b, 10f.; also 1986e). Minsky is precise in saying that the problem is not the shadowy nature of this activity, but rather the fact that, like all banking innovations, it multiplies the number of claims on the underlying wealth. This multiplication comes in the form of backup lines of credit promised by the core banks to the peripheral banks: when losses hit the fringes, they will turn to their commercial banks for support. The shadow banks of the 2008 crisis did exactly this (Mehrling 2010; Grad, Mehrling, and Neilson 2011; Mehrling et al. 2013).

Actors in the financial capitalist system adjust their portfolios, sometimes creating new patterns of financial usage in order to do so. Financial innovation reflects the tension between a private push for expansion and a public push for restraint. The resulting evolution is a strong force, Minsky saw, toward instability.

\* \* \*

Schumpeter is absent in the 1960 study – perhaps Minsky felt that the audience was likely to share the inclinations of his own cohort of graduate students at Harvard. He sought instead to reach them with practical questions of policy. His dissertation work on accelerator–multiplier models, a conventional tool for economic modeling at the time, had been published in a 1957 article (1957b) and provided a language through which he could try to get his unconventional vision across. Unnamed, Schumpeter's influence on that vision is nonetheless clearly visible; it is a world where economic change is expressed through financial change. As finance responds to the needs of entrepreneurs, the organization of financial practices changes:

> In a dynamic free enterprise economy the financial system undergoes changes. Financial institutions, financial relations among the various classes of economic units and institutions, and the relative size of financial institutions all change. Economic growth is usually accompanied by financial innovation; new types of financial institutions and instruments are invented and put to use. (1964a, 173)

The young Minsky was confident in the capacity of an innovative capitalist system to weed out the innovations that contributed to instability – a prior that would later have to be discarded, confronted with contrary experience beginning in 1966. But from the point of view of 1960, it seemed to Minsky that market forces were enough to ensure that a system that allowed for changes in the patterns of finance would nonetheless tend toward some kind of stability.

> [F]inancial evolution is a response to the growth pattern, and whether the new financing techniques and relationships perish or survive depends upon how they affect the functioning of the economy. Financial innovations which are believed to abet financial instability soon disappear or are reduced in importance either as a result of market processes or legislation. Examples which can be cited are "accommodation paper" and "low" margin requirements on stock exchange collateral. Financial innovations such as consumer installment credit which are related to the financing of profitable growing industries expand and become a permanent part of the financial framework. (1964a, 174)

Subsequent crises would render this sanguine view untenable, but the more general point would stand: financial patterns change over time, so that knowledge about the structure of the system becomes obsolete. The enduring lesson of the 1960 study is that economic knowledge is not a permanent, unchanging resolution of social questions for all time. Rather, the lessons of experience are written into the changing institutions. But experience is not a perfect guide to the future:

> [W]e do not expect one period of sustained growth to be just like another. In particular we expect that lessons are learned, that legislation exists and institutions have been created which [protect] the economy against the typical financial crises that have been observed. But this learning from the past can result in a type of "Maginot Line" mentality, in which the economy is left vulnerable to new kinds of destabilizing financial reactions. (1964a, 177)

The argument is, in the end, a case for a study of society that is in sharp contrast to the norms of the economics profession, then and now. It is an object of study that is changing underfoot, in which interventions based on experience, whether they originate from the private impulse toward gain or from the public reflex toward stability, are limited by their authors' inability to anticipate the future. Minsky's is a social world that is beset by inescapable novelty, where there is simply nothing that can be done to eliminate the necessity of change. We are far from the economist's equilibrium.

* * *

## The financial instability hypothesis

No economist writing in the years following the Depression could ignore the cyclical aspect of the economic system: that the fortunes of an entire society sometimes rise and fall as one. From his days as a graduate student, the question that motivated Minsky's financial understanding of US capitalism was its potential for instability. At that time, the only reference point was backward, to 1929 and the Depression that followed. The series of financial crises that unfolded from 1966 forward, however, offered fresh examples with which to elaborate the theory. Crisis seemed to grow out of, and bring an end to, a boom. Minsky was drawn to focus on these sudden stops: why does a run of prosperous times come crashing to a halt, rather than easing into a period of bad times?

\* \* \*

Without naming Schumpeter, the opening sections of the 1960 study place the financial system, the money markets, centrally as the "headquarters of capitalism," organized around the structure of payment commitments faced by all actors; that financial structure changes over time, interacting with the changing needs of enterprise. This groundwork distinguishes Minsky's work, and allows him to paint a vivid picture of financial crisis. Systemic financial distress could arise simply as a result of some widespread decline in incomes (due to war, for example) with no role for financial interactions. What is more interesting, however, is a crisis in which some initial disturbance is amplified, "one in which the internal relations within the financial system generate the financial crisis."

> An economic unit, for unexplained reasons, finds itself in financial difficulty. It sells assets, borrows, and draws upon its deposit accounts in an effort to avoid financial distress, but to no avail. As a result of the financial distress of this unit it defaults on its payments, and economic units which own its liabilities make financial losses. The impact by way of defaults and decreases in the value of its liabilities, upon other economic units, places some of these units in financial difficulties. These units resort to borrowing, selling assets, and making withdrawals from their deposits. In spite of these defensive operations these units end up in financial distress. A cumulative rising tide of financial distress spreads through the community. There is no pressure on the financial resources of any unit due to a decrease in income; the

entire financial pressure that is generated is due to the effect of the financial distress of some units upon the financial position of other units. (1964a, 263)

Minsky had said in 1954 that to understand crisis, the liquidity phenomenon needed to be incorporated into Schumpeter's view. Now he had a statement of that phenomenon, and a sense of how it could cause distress to become systemic. An initial disturbance, the nature of which is of little importance, makes it difficult for one actor to fulfill its payment commitments. The financial structure connecting it to other actors causes the disturbance to spread through purely financial means, even to actors unaffected by the initial fall in income. Desperate efforts to meet payment commitments are insufficient, and crisis becomes systemic.

*　*　*

Crisis is distinguished not so much by disturbance as by the amplification of small disturbance. "In a fragile financial system[,] continued normal functioning can be disrupted by some not unusual event" (1977b, 139). A panic can be set in motion by events that, on another day, might pass without major consequences. If the precipitating event need not be exceptional, then the theory of crisis that is needed is one that addresses the unfolding consequences of those not unusual events, and why a crisis sometimes results, and sometimes does not. Quite different from a theory of an economy that rests on random shocks that arise from without, this is a theory of the systemic susceptibility of the capitalist financial structure, at times to even the smallest of shocks.

Minsky was able to give an elegant and persuasive answer, one that makes use of his vision of a financial system made up of evolving financial connections among bank-like economic units. Good times, he saw, lead to systemic changes in financial structure. The opportunities of an economic boom, we have seen, lead households and businesses to make changes in their patterns of borrowing and lending – investing and saving – so as to free up funds for the pursuit of those opportunities. The effect of this cyclical evolution, however, is to make the system more fragile, until a small disturbance – one that might go unremarked during a period of robust finance – can push the entire financial system into crisis. Memorably: *stability is destabilizing*.

This "financial instability hypothesis" was to become one of Minsky's most enduring contributions. Minsky said it many ways, in many different formulations, over his career (for example, 1957b; 1977f; 1978d; 1982d; 1991b; 1994). (I suppose my favorite statement is one of the earliest: "The financing of an expansion by increasing velocity tends to create a situation in which both a financial crisis and a deep depression are possible" (1957a, 186). The reader curious to take on Minsky in the original might start by comparing that statement to a later one like that of (1982d).) The crux of the theory remained constant over the years: the financial patterns of the boom pave the way for crisis. The financial instability hypothesis poses a serious problem for those, like Minsky, who wish to make financial capitalism work. Stable growth of employment and output is the goal of policy, and the implication of Keynesian economics seemed to be that good management could provide such stability. But if stability is destabilizing, if good times always end in crisis, management may be futile. The policies that bring prosperity also bring crisis.

* * *

How a financial crisis could spread and become systemic was clear in Minsky's language. But not every fall in income led to a widespread financial crisis. Sometimes the disturbance spread uncontrollably; sometimes it died out on its own. In 1929–33 it had been the former, an initial disturbance in the stock market leading eventually to the closure of the entire banking system. But since then, no comparable crisis had taken place. Minsky had been focusing on the Great Depression from the beginning; now his charge from the Commission on Money and Credit was to ask whether "it" could happen again. The possibility that the financial structure could amplify a disturbance clarified Minsky's understanding of the 1929 crash:

> There is no need to assume that the triggering event, the downturn of August 1929, is significantly different in its origins and in its initial strength from the other observed peacetime contractions. ... What has to be explained is why an unexceptional downturn had serious financial repercussions which other recessions did not have. The explanation that will be advanced is that the financial environment within which the contraction beginning in August 1929 took place was different from the financial environment of the earlier contracts in the period after 1919. This changed financial environment was the result of both the manner in which the sustained boom of the 1920s was financed and the effect upon financial variables of the expectation that sustained growth was inevitable. (1964a, 205)

The stock market crash of 1929, then, was amplified because the financial environment had grown more fragile during the preceding boom. Once the system is fragile, a crisis is easily triggered: if the fuel is explosive, the source of the spark makes little difference. The conclusion is powerful, and was one that Minsky would carry with him to all of his future projects. The heart of his 1960 study is an attempt to answer the problem from his 1954 dissertation, an answer that opens up an entire line of thinking: how can we understand the changing patterns of finance as they become more fragile? The expansiveness of the problem made it a grand adventure indeed; it was a way of taking on the Schumpeterian challenge of understanding capitalism as a whole. The ingredients – changing financial usages and a central role for payments – were simple enough, and drawn from institutional experience. Minsky was compelled by his vision, and it seemed to yield clear insights and a way forward.

* * *

The financial instability hypothesis was a powerful indictment of financial capitalism, as well as of the policy and academic elites with a stake in that system. From the beginning of his career, Minsky, from the margins of the profession, sought to express his critique in the language of academic economics. An early version of the financial instability hypothesis is visible in Minsky's doctoral dissertation (1954; Delli Gatti and Gallegati 1997). Already in that first work, in which he tries to show how crisis can arise in the accelerator–multiplier framework that was in vogue at the time, there was a clear tension between what Minsky wanted to say about financial capitalism, and the language in which he was trying to say it.

Minsky never compromised on the theoretical underpinnings of his vision; nor did he ever give up on attempting to communicate with economists, despite their differences in perspective. It will be the work of much of the rest of this book to understand the mechanisms of financial capitalism that contribute to instability, especially in chapters 3 and 5; as well as the nature of the incompatibility of Minsky's theory with academic economics, especially in chapters 4 and 7; and how Minsky thought about the question of managing an inherently unstable system, especially in chapter 6. But in a way the translation problem is already clear. The hypothesis depends on two big ideas – that everyone is like a bank, and that financial patterns change – neither of which can easily be expressed in an economic language that leaves little room for payment, and that supposes a tendency toward equilibrium.

## Coherence

The financial instability hypothesis says that a market economy with a financial system will, from time to time, explode into crisis. One might reasonably expect that these discrete events, with bankruptcies of major financial institutions and significant intervention by authorities, and not infrequently followed by deep recessions and unemployment, would be of singular importance to observers of society. Financial crises can be counted on to provide sufficiently dramatic circumstances and colorful characters to receive narrative treatment, for example Adam McKay's comedy *The Big Short* or Charles Ferguson's documentary *Inside Job*, about 2008, or Thomas Love Peacock's poem "Pan in Town," about the 1825 crisis (Hicks 1989). Minsky felt that crisis was significant enough to render financial capitalism "inherently flawed" ([1986e] 2008, 320).

The passage of time, however, makes it possible to discount the importance of past financial instability, despite its regularity and even repetitiveness. Indeed, the time between two crises must be long enough for changes in the instruments and patterns of the financial system to occur, an imperfect integration of society's memory of financial trauma. "Expectation formation takes into account that 'The world has changed' and that 'They won't let it happen,' even though agents are not sure who 'they' are and what 'they' will do" (1989a, 181).

Minsky was often puzzled that his fellow economists seemed to attach so little importance to crisis. Responding to Arrow and Hahn's (1971) treatment of markets – representative then as now of economic orthodoxy – which unlike Minsky's has little place for cash flows, or for financial innovation, he asks whether the optimistic conclusions they draw about the stability of decentralized exchange will carry over once finance has been accounted for. Arrow and Hahn see decentralized markets tending smoothly toward equilibrium, toward a balance of supply and demand; by discounting the financial substance that goes with real markets, they likewise discount the importance of crisis. Where his colleagues see a normally efficient system occasionally disrupted from without, Minsky saw a system whose normal behavior gives rise to bouts of incoherence.

Coherence is Minsky's name for a disposition of resources that matches supply and demand, which a decentralized market normally achieves (1980b). It would hardly be possible for anyone to defend the market system if some kind of coherence did not usually prevail. But it must also be conceded that episodes of financial crisis, depression, and large-scale unemployment are clear evidence of occasional incoherence. Minsky was a sharp critic of his colleagues' perspective, which recognized such phenomena only as minor disruptions to an otherwise coherent tendency toward equilibrium. The financial instability hypothesis, by contrast, says that though financial capitalism is not usually incoherent, it nonetheless tends to crisis (1988d). Incoherence arises normally out of coherence. To Minsky, this was a challenge that economists had to take up; it was the central question of financial capitalism.

When a boom reaches its end, robust finance has given way to fragile finance (though this may not yet be widely known) and sudden disruptions become possible. Business as usual – when disruptions are isolated and quickly absorbed and forgotten, so that equilibrium seems like a plausible metaphor – comes to an end. "Incoherent behavior occurs when the reaction to a disturbance amplifies rather than dampens the initial disturbance" (1977b, 140). In a fragile financial environment, default and failure are a chain reaction, spawning more defaults and more failures. The devastating unemployment that followed the 1929 crash provided an object lesson: incoherence must be reined in.

Minsky thought that public institutions could put bounds on the fluctuations of financial capitalism so as to limit the costs of incoherence, and he thought that economic theory could and should give some guidance as to how this could be done. "Hopefully understanding how a capitalist economy behaves will give us knowledge that will enable us to control and change it so that its most perverse characteristics are either eliminated or attenuated" (1978d, 7). Financial arrangements alternate between coherence and incoherence, and capitalism is therefore indeed flawed, but it might nevertheless be safely operated. To have any hope of doing so, however, a theory was needed that connected the boom to the bust, coherence to incoherence, normal times to crisis times.

This was Minsky's intellectual ambition, and in the chapters that follow I lay out such a theory. That theory also sheds some light on even more expansive questions about capitalism itself. For even if the economy can be steered toward coherence, we may not be satisfied with the results. "A coherent economy need not be a just economy" (1977d, 26). The passage of time, the changing of social circumstances, mean that our answers to such questions must change: "That capitalism is flawed does not necessarily mean that one rejects capitalism … [T]here are varieties of capitalism. The question may very well be which variety is better, not necessarily for all time, but for now" (1978d, 21).

## Before and after the "moment"

In the Russian debt crisis of 1998, Paul McCulley, then of Pacific Investments and later of PIMCO, used his platform to call attention to the relevance of Minsky's work for the sudden eruption of financial instability in a crisis, giving us the "Minsky moment." The precise date of that coinage seems be lost, but McCulley used it again as the tech bubble ended a few years later (McCulley 2001). The phrase made the rounds once again in 2007 and 2008, as the so-called subprime crisis began and spread. It does not seem inappropriate to identify that moment in the financial cycle with Hyman Minsky – it is the point when the exuberance of the boom finally tips over into panic, into widespread anxiety about financial conditions. In 1998, as in 2001 and 2008, it is the time when the world turns to Minsky for answers, and surely in the next financial crisis it will do so again.

\* \* \*

The study for the Commission on Money and Credit had been an opportunity for Minsky to put his vision to work in a substantial investigation. He had the freedom to spell out his theoretical perspective from first principles, and sought to use it to find an audience for what he understood to be a new type of economic analysis. That analysis led to insight into the nature of the last big crisis – the 1929 crash had a huge effect because of changes in the pattern of financial usages during the period that had preceded the crisis. For Minsky, the analysis was not the end of the story: his perspective also had implications for how policy-makers might respond. If crisis is not about the precipitating event, but rather about fragile structures that amplify it, then the job of the central bank must be to understand that fragility and anticipate it:

> [T]he central bank, for instance, should have stretched its responsibility and made it possible to maintain asset values on the stock

exchange after some initial decline in stock prices in 1929. For by 1929 the inflated prices of common stocks had been built into the asset structure of the financial system, so that any severe decline of stock prices threatened a financial collapse. (1964a, 376)

The liability structures that had emerged to support the financing of stock market positions over the years preceding the crash of 1929 were built with assumptions about stock prices; a stock market decline in such a fragile situation would be likely to spill over into crisis. The central bank, Minsky concluded, should even have reached beyond the normal bounds of its authority to prevent this from happening. The conclusion was in stark contrast to those of monetarism, which was to dominate academic discourse from the 1960s to the 1990s. The monetarists argued for a central bank constrained by rules, deprived of discretion; Minsky was making the case for intervention, intervention not only unconstrained by rules but in contravention of them:

> By the end of the 1920s, unless the central bank were willing to "throw away" all the rules of the central banking game as understood at that time, in times of crisis, the commercial banks were not in a very liquid position. ... By the rules of the game "as understood at that time" I mean the use of the discount window for restricted types of assets and perhaps open market purchase of government securities. It is obvious ... that in the 1928–29 period the central bank, to protect the liquidity of the commercial banking system, should have been considering the need to provide refinancing for the vast amount of paper related to "purchasing and carrying securities." (1964a, 323)

When the financial system, and thus the capitalist system of which it is the center, requires stabilization, the rules are of little importance, for what value are the rules if the system collapses? The 1929 crisis in particular, he thought, and financial crises in general, were not inevitable. They demanded appropriate, and timely, intervention: "Of course even if widespread financial distress exists, so widespread that it will soon degenerate into a financial crisis, there is no need for the financial crisis to take place. Appropriate action by the central bank and the government can abort any financial crisis" (1964a, 181).

* * *

Though we might accept the label "Minsky moment," it would be a mistake to make Minsky's work out to be a theory for crisis only. The apex of a crisis is the moment when the excesses of speculation are revealed, when the boom is shown to have been overdone. That speculation originates in the patterns of cash flows and changing financial usages that led up to it. But Minsky moments are not isolated, are not blips on an otherwise smooth and stable path of economic growth. To the contrary, crises arise normally as part of financial capitalism. Minsky's is a theory that shows how that happens.

During his career, Minsky welcomed the attention to his work that each crisis brought, and each time, he took the opportunity to sketch for a newly attentive audience the outlines of a theory that showed how the bust would follow from the boom. An economic theory that ignores the matching of cash inflows with cash outflows, that ignores the change in financial arrangements over time, could never go far toward an understanding of crisis.

In this chapter we have seen the main features of financial capitalism as Minsky understood it, and how, in such a system, stability leads to instability. In the next chapter, we look more closely at the role of patterns of financial behavior in that process.

# 3

# *A payments theory of finance*

## Capitalism and payment

Minsky gives pride of place to finance in understanding capitalism: "Capitalism is essentially a financial system" (1967a, 33; also Mehrling 1999). We have begun to see the consequences of that idea, by following him in thinking of each economic actor as managing cash inflows and outflows, and managing a portfolio of assets and liabilities. This was sturdy enough ground on which to give a first statement of Minsky's financial stability hypothesis.

To connect Minsky's ideas to patterns more specific to the financial system, of his own time and of ours, some elaboration of the theory will be needed, which is the work of this chapter. There is little that is truly new in financial innovation, as we shall see, and Minsky was able to identify and illustrate, repeatedly, several basic financial mechanisms that played out many times through his career. These constitute the language that Minsky used to describe the behavior of the financial system, a language not entirely consonant with that of other economists. If Minsky's language is not quite enough to predict a crisis, it is certainly enough to illuminate. I venture to call the mechanisms described in this chapter a theory of finance, organized around the defining act of *payment*.

We might start by noting, with Hicks (1989), that it is reasonable to divide every market transaction into three parts: the agreement of both parties, the delivery of the goods, and payment in money. The agreement must come first, but the other two parts can come in either order, and can be separated in time. It is only in the simplest of cash transactions that payment comes immediately. For any large or commercial transaction, spot payment is not expected; today even most retail transactions are electronic and are not, in practice, settled immediately. The generic market transaction, that is, involves the creation of a debt to be settled later in money.

This, for Minsky, is what it means for capitalism to be essentially financial. Every market transaction creates a debt, a payment commitment, a promise to deliver money. Any sale creates a liability for the buyer, who is expected eventually to pay, and an asset for the seller, who expects eventually to be paid. All transactions share this form, regardless of what is being bought and sold. The totality of assets and liabilities is thus the commitments to pay arising from the totality of market transactions (1964a). The financial structure is therefore the starting place not just for an analysis of the financial system itself, but for an analysis of the entire capitalist system.

\* \* \*

The 1964–5 academic year brought political unrest to the Berkeley campus, in a series of contests between students and administration that marked a key point in the unfolding of left politics in the US over the remainder of the decade (Unger 1974). Minsky makes no mention of these events in his publications; he seems rather to have directed his political energies toward his work on poverty, mentioned in the previous chapter. That year also brought an opportunity to the young professor: service as chair of the University's Institute of Business and Economic Research, and the task of editing a volume on the state's banking system, *California Banking in a Growing Economy: 1946–1975*.

Minsky contributed a paper to the book, and as editor wrote an introduction to the entire volume (1965b; 1965c). The economic relevance of the book has surely faded: the papers, organized at the initiative of the state's governor, were a first foray into the financial system of what was then a rapidly growing and changing regional economy. Minsky is not alone among the contributors in remarking on the lack of data on their subject, and the guesswork necessitated by these limitations. But such work on the California banking system brought a new set of questions, and Minsky learned something by adapting his analytical approach to the subject at hand.

As always for Minsky, the starting point was cash commitments; what was new in the California study was that those payments crossed a political boundary. In his dissertation and in the 1960 study,

Minsky's focus had been on cash commitments between unitary actors: a bank and a firm, for example. Such actors, represented by their balance sheets, were indivisible; what happened inside of them had been of no interest. To study California, however, required an adaptation of the analytical frame: it was both accounting unit, making and receiving money payments, and aggregate, encompassing the actors within it:

> A check drawn on a California bank and deposited for collection in an out-of-state bank requires the California bank to make a payment in reserve money. Symmetrically, a check deposited in a California bank drawn on an out-of-state bank brings reserve money into the California bank. The ebb and flow of payments on current account and on capital account, over time, results in the net change in the reserves of banks within the state. (1965b, 93)

A region, such as the state of California, finds its place in Minsky's framework not primarily as a political unit, but as an accounting entity, a group of actors, acting independently but viewed collectively, making and accepting cash commitments. The business activity that determines the fortunes of those within California relative to those without can be understood by looking at the payment commitments made across that boundary, payments both incoming and outgoing. As the money market was the headquarters of US capitalism, California's banking system, then, was the headquarters of capitalism for that regional, internal market. Unlike a nation-state with an independent monetary policy, however, California had to make do with policy made for the US as a whole:

> Basically the monetary system of a region is similar to that of a country under a gold standard so strict that there is no room for an independent monetary policy. Deposits in the central bank, the reserve money of the country, are the analogues to gold when a region is compared with a country. That demand deposits are freely exchanged for currency (a form of reserve money), and that a dollar is a dollar throughout the country, further increases the similarity of a regional monetary system with a strict gold standard national monetary system. (1965b, 95)

This understanding of California's position in the United States would later inform Minsky's picture of the US's position in the world. This took the form of a tiered categorization of the international flows of payment that make up the balance of payment (1979; 1986a; 1986b; 1986f; 1988b). I can only gesture to this work, and connect it to the study on California banking, when Minsky first begins to think about cross-border payments.

\* \* \*

The portfolios of chapter 2 are really portfolios of payment commitments: assets are collections of payments to be received, liabilities are collections of payments to be made (1954; 1962; 1987c; 1991c). A portfolio decision is an expression of what commitments an actor wishes to be party to. In choosing what positions to hold, it is configuring its set of cash in- and outflows, and doing this as a bank would, so that funds coming in can be used to meet commitments. Payment, the act of fulfilling such a commitment, is the starting point for a theory of finance.

Where there is payment, there is money, and money will play a role in the discussions that follow. But beginning with the act of payment rather than with the object of money helped Minsky avoid getting bogged down in trying to define and understand money *per se*: "To examine the relation between money and financial instability it is necessary to look at 'money on the wing'" (1964b, 328). Better, that is, to focus on money as a flow, as the means by which payment is made, the means by which debts are settled, than to dwell on trying to say precisely what is or is not money. I follow Minsky's lead in starting with what money *does*, coming only later to what money *is*.

\* \* \*

Minsky's editorial role on the California book was an opportunity to collaborate. He wrote a substantive summary of each paper for the introduction to the volume; learning something from each. Summarizing a paper by Richard E. Towey on the payments mechanism, Minsky writes that it

> investigates a rapidly changing aspect of banking usually not considered in discussion of banking policy and structure. Banks do the mechanical job of operating the economy's payments mechanism. They do it so well that the general public, and even sophisticated commentators, usually are not aware that there is any problem involved in making payments, especially payments at a distance. The growth of the economy, the rise in the importance of demand deposits relative to currency in making payments, and the increased complexity of the financial system have combined to generate a rapidly growing flood of checks. The purely mechanical problem of processing the checks threatened to lead to difficulties until banks adjusted their techniques

and adopted sophisticated, computerized operations. These changes in
the mechanics of banking potentially have broad implications for the
structure of the banking system and the public regulatory agencies.
(1965c, 15)

Towey's attention to this normally unseen aspect of the financial
system, the processes for check-clearing, connected closely with
Minsky's own time as an observer at a New York money-market
broker, described in (1957a). Minsky saw in the mechanical, normally
uneventful day-to-day of financial capitalism a source of new information about the operation of the system, and a hint of what
important conclusions might be drawn from that evidence.

* * *

Payment is the characteristic social act in a financial capitalist
system. The payments made by one actor are the payments received
by another, and every actor makes and receives payments over
time. Minsky understood the financial structure of a market society
to be a network of interlocking payment commitments, made in
the past and maturing in the present, and made in the present and
stretching into the future (1980a). His work was to describe the
patterns and behaviors around payment that animate this network,
and that explain its normal functioning as well as they explain
its notable pathologies. These mechanisms are the subject of the
sections that follow.

## Survival constraint

The most important mechanism of financial capitalism is the one
that gives debt its force: the requirement to pay. The statement
that one must pay one's debts is so implicit in the logic of our
market society that it seems at first to be without content. The
debtor who fails to pay is assumed to feel guilt and shame, and
such a reaction seems entirely natural, for to skip out on one's
debts is to be a cheat and a thief. On closer inspection, however,
the obligation to pay is far more nuanced: Graeber (2011) uses the
moral confusion prompted by this very question to motivate his
history of debt. Indeed the requirement to pay is historically and
socially contingent; it is a feature of how market society works,
today, not a feature of humanity or of social life more generally.
Minsky called this requirement the *survival constraint*: debts must

be paid when due. As best as I can determine, recognition of the explanatory power of the survival constraint for financial instability should be credited to Minsky, but the idea must have come in part from his studies with his undergraduate professor at Chicago, Henry Simons.

Simons lamented the loss of the gold standard, as well as the contradictions of the encroaching penchant for monetary management empowered by Keynes. The crux of his liberal vision is a decentralized market system as the best defense of freedom, freedom both from monopoly concentrations of industrial power *and* from socialist concentrations of political power. For this to be possible, the market must be made to work without constant intervention.

In an influential essay, Simons offers a series of theoretical monetary arrangements that would, from his perspective, promote stable finance without constant intervention. We might, he imagined adventurously, abandon fixed-money contracts altogether: it would be impossible, under such a system, to commit oneself to making a payment fixed in money terms, in the future, or to accept such a commitment. Or failing that, we might allow fixed-money contracts only in perpetuity: one can accept a commitment to be paid a specific amount only by giving up the right ever to demand payment at a specific time. Or, coming nearer to practicality, we might accept only long-term contracts, or at the very least, finally, a reduced reliance on short-term contracts (Simons 1948).

The lure of these monetary proposals is that they reduce the force of the requirement to pay. If it is impossible to commit a fixed sum of money, Simons thought, then entrepreneurs would be more free to pursue their visions, without the yoke of a looming obligation to their creditors. Payment would come in the form of a residual, whatever funds were left over, just as the owners of equities are entitled to a share of a company's net assets. If it is impossible to commit to payment at a specific moment in time, the effect is much the same: even if a specific sum must be paid, if the date of that payment never arrives, it does little to bring anxiety to the owner of a business.

Simons's intention, to be sure, was to defend capitalism as a bastion of liberty. The most important freedom in that vision was the freedom of the entrepreneur from their lenders, and his proposals aim to protect that freedom by eliminating payment as we know it. It is a capitalism quite different from the one we have known (Minsky 1985b). Minsky's vision was very different, and so I leave aside the possibilities of this entrepreneurial world.

Where the teacher Simons was Utopian, aiming to free borrowers from the obligation to pay, his student Minsky was pragmatic, aiming to deal with the fact that they must. Still, Minsky starts from just where Simons leaves off: the fact that, like it or not, cash commitments are fixed in time and amount. The requirement to pay is the survival constraint: "[I]n order to survive, the firm must satisfy the condition that the initial cash plus the receipts minus the costs payable to that date are greater than zero" ([1954] 2000, 96). Minsky abandons the phrase "survival constraint" after his dissertation, but this is because he builds the idea more deeply into his thinking, not because he gives it up: "[A]side from units in the monetary sector, the cash balance of a unit at any date sets the maximum amount by which the sum of its money payments can exceed the sum of its money receipts from that date on. One of the determinants of the behavior of any private economic unit is the need to satisfy this 'cash box' condition" (1964a, 237f.).

* * *

If the set of assets and liabilities, the topology of cash commit-ments, defines an evolving financial structure, then it is the survival constraint that tests that structure at each moment in time (Mehrling 2010). Evolving financial usages give institutional form to financial capitalism, while the need to make good on promises to pay urges actors into behavior that sustains it. The California study, without using the phrase, nonetheless uses the logic of the survival constraint to set business activity in motion. Minsky uses that logic to sketch a model about what future the state's banking system might expect:

> Mortgages, state and local debt, corporate bonds, and deposits in California savings and loan associations all generate payments which are committed by contracts. On mortgages and bonds the payments are contractual, whereas deposits in savings and loan associations are demand liabilities: even the interest paid on such deposits is usually credited to the accounts and paid in money only when "demanded." ... As an offset to the contractual payments made on account of debts, there are the contractual and contingent receipts which California persons, financial institutions, and business enterprises receive per period because of the ownership of assets based outside of California. ... The assumption that California is a net debtor state means that these receipts are smaller than the contractual payments which must be made. (1965b, 130f.)

California actors make commitments, that is, to the rest of the world; at the same time actors in the rest of the world make commitments in California. Some of these commitments are fixed in time and amount, like bond and mortgage payments; others are payable upon the creditor's demand. As of 1965, Minsky continues, outgoing payment commitments were being met with the help of continued lending from out-of-state. The expansion was sustainable so long as the survival constraint did not bind and the state could keep its cash commitments. But a greater preponderance of sight liabilities, payable on demand, meant that a change in the state's prospects could trigger a withdrawal of financing, and a sudden tightening of the survival constraint.

The core of this argument – the need to match money received with money promised, as a bank does – comes from Minsky's adherence to his analytical frame: by viewing California as an accounting entity, and attending to the business activity generating payments in and out, he expanded the range of his analytical language. He had said in the 1960 study for the Commission on Money and Credit that he was developing a new approach to economic analysis, and the 1965 California study seemed to bear out his priors. The structure of his argument was to leave a more permanent impression on Minsky's thinking than the content: it gave him a way to think about how the survival constraint was being met.

As he typically did when considering the stability of a financial structure, Minsky found that California's financial patterns were unsustainable: he saw that California, in the aggregate, relied on incoming investment payments from elsewhere to meet its payment commitments. If this inflow were to slow, California's banks would face trouble. He was politic in presenting this conclusion in the 1965 study, which had been commissioned by the state's governor: "[a]ppropriate public policies are needed which slow the withdrawal of stimuli" (1965b, 134). But in a talk two years later, ensconced in his new post at Washington University in St Louis, he stated his conclusion more bluntly: "Only the continued accelerated flow of out-of-state investment funds to the state has made this burden feasible: California has been playing a 'Ponzi' game with the rest of the country" (1967b, 272). The label "Ponzi" was to become one of Minsky's most durable brands.

* * *

Each actor, then, has its set of positions, its assets and liabilities, recorded together on its balance sheet. Those commitments that are properly financial are two-sided: for one actor, the borrower, they are a liability; for the other, the lender, they are an asset. Liabilities commit a borrower to make payments; the borrower thus faces a potentially binding survival constraint when the moment to pay arrives. One failed payment may not be the end of the trouble, though. One borrower's missed payment deprives their lender of a cash inflow. But if this lender is in turn a borrower from another actor, they face a survival constraint of their own. If the expected cash inflow is missing, the lender might miss their own outgoing payment.

In Minsky's financial capitalism, the balancing of these two flows is a problem faced by every economic actor: "Each economic unit – be it a business firm, household, financial institution, or government – is a money-in-money-out device" (1980a, 212). The survival constraint is a statement of the necessity of succeeding at that task. A chronic inability to meet the household survival constraint out of wages, for example, precisely describes Minsky's conception of poverty. Financial distress can originate either from insufficient inflows or from excessive outflows, and in a variety of ways – income may fall short, a debtor may default, assets may fall in market value, a contingent liability (such as an insurance contract) may become current – but in all cases, the proximate source of distress, the reason for urgency, is the survival constraint (1964a).

The word "survival" captures the urgency well. That label, dropped after Minsky's dissertation, was used there to mean avoiding bankruptcy. Regardless of what other difficulties a firm might face, it is default on payment commitments that triggers legal action by creditors. A failing firm might well limp along if it can still make payment; an otherwise healthy firm might be brought quickly to the brink if it suddenly becomes unable to pay. The urgency is even more profound when thinking of household cash flows. One might reasonably note (though Minsky did not do so in as many words) that in a market society in which a household's basic needs – for food, health, and shelter – are met in the market, the survival constraint conveys urgency in a more literal and sinister sense: one must pay in order to survive.

That urgency, the need to meet the commitment that is due today, may well justify compromising future payments. The 2008 crisis affords numerous examples of behavior guided by the survival constraint. A simple observation is that, in the real-estate boom that preceded the crisis, the wide prevalence of loan applications

with minor fraud could go unnoticed, because they did not necessarily lead borrowers to miss payments: "Such loans could stay
comfortably under the radar, because many borrowers made
payments on time" (FCIC 2011, 160). Sometimes support for meeting
the survival constraint was written into the terms of the contract.
A notable innovation in the boom in mortgage finance was in
marketing new adjustment patterns for adjustable-rate mortgages.
One of the more consequential was the issuance of adjustable-rate
mortgages (ARMs) with low initial "teaser" rates. Such "Balloon
ARMs" were a way of avoiding the borrowers' survival constraint:

> "As homes got less and less affordable, you would adjust for the
> affordability in the mortgage because you couldn't really adjust
> people's income," Andrew Davidson, the president of Andrew
> Davidson & Co. and a veteran of the mortgage markets, told the
> FCIC. Lenders qualified borrowers at low teaser rates, with little
> thought to what might happen when rates reset. Hybrid ARMs
> became the workhorses of the subprime securitization market. (FCIC
> 2011, 106)

The survival constraint is simply stated – it is the requirement
of a market system that debts be settled in money. Its effect is to
create a sense of urgency for the borrower as the date approaches,
and anxiety and fear about the possibility that funds will not be
available. The survival constraint also implies, of course, that
sometimes payment will not in fact be made, that those fears will
be realized, and so it can significantly shape behavior.

## Position-making and cash kickers

Businesses and people must meet their cash commitments as they
come due; they must pay their debts as they mature. How will
they do so? What will be the immediate source of funds that gives
lenders, as well as borrowers themselves, confidence to think that
payment will in fact be forthcoming when the hour arrives? The
question was central as Minsky observed developments in the
financial markets, especially in the mid-1970s.

Though he had lost the phrase "survival constraint," Minsky kept
his focus on the moment of payment. At that moment, where do
people turn for cash? He finds a systematic answer in the banking
concept of *making position*. "The position making instrument is that

instrument which will be sold (be it an asset or a liability) if the unit requires cash" (1974c, 272). The position-making instrument may vary across time and across different types of institution, but it will not be random or arbitrary, because the need to make position is one that is always being anticipated.

Banks must maintain an intense focus on this need; a bank that cannot meet its obligations will be quickly without customers. Writing about bank examination, Minsky says "a bank first lends or invests and then 'finds' the cash to cover whatever cash drains arise" (1975d, 154; also 1984a). Bankers must remain keenly aware of the timing of payment commitments as they approach, and so, in general, they do not enter into such commitments without a sense of where the funds to meet them will come from and when they will become available. The bank finds the needed cash – it makes position – by drawing down its own cash balances, by selling other assets, or by borrowing; this position-making is the "essential operation" of a bank (1975d, 154). (A bank must make position when its depositors demand their funds, or when its short-term debts come due, or when its borrowers unexpectedly default. This is quite different, it should be said, from its need to fund loans, which a bank can do by issuing deposits to the borrower. It is only when these deposits must be made good in the form of money, as when completing a payment on behalf of the depositor, that the question of position-making arises.)

If position-making is put in sharp relief in banks, it is not by any means limited to them: it is a version of the problem of cash flows faced by all economic actors who must, like banks, meet their cash commitments. No borrower enters into a commitment without some kind of a plan – imagined more or less realistically – for how to make position: "When a financial contract is created, both the buyer (lender) and the seller (borrower) have scenarios in mind by which the seller acquires the cash which is needed to fulfil the terms of the contract. In a typical situation there is a primary and some secondary or fallback sources of cash" (1980a, 213).

* * *

Minsky was already thinking about position-making when looking at California banks. If cash inflows from out-of-state were cut short, for example by a withdrawal of federal government spending, then borrowers in the state would be pressed to find new sources to meet their payment commitments. The manner in which they did so would determine the financial effects of the change in business. Each group has institutional patterns and arrangements for meeting the survival constraint when it binds:

> The existence of specialized agencies which enable savings and loan associations to meet large-scale cash drains without a dumping of earning assets, means that such financial flows can be weathered. The commercial banks, by selling their national assets and borrowing from the Federal Reserve Bank, can meet the drains imposed upon them by the out-of-state payments by savings and loan associations whose deposits they hold. (1965b, 133)

Taking the state of California as the unit of analysis provided some insight into the mechanism of position-making. The survival constraint does sometimes bind; otherwise it would be no kind of constraint at all. One way to meet it is for an actor to fall back on another as it works to make position, through borrowing from or selling to that actor. This shifts the burden of the survival constraint to that other actor. In the California case, government agencies supporting the savings and loan banks served that purpose. The shift is successful if the latter are not bound by their own survival constraint; that is, if they can stop the cash drain out of their own resources. The interposition of the state of California as a level of analysis allowed a more elaborate hierarchy to take shape.

\* \* \*

What will be the fallback sources of cash? "The instruments and financial markets used in position-making change over time, and at any one time not all banks will make position in the same way" (1975d, 154). Thus position-making is not an unchanging usage of a specific instrument; it is a behavioral pattern that takes different forms in different contexts. This does not, however, prevent some generalizations. One pattern, important to Minsky, has to do with an actor's ability to make position out of incoming cash flows. Minsky divided actors into three categories. A unit could have money on hand – cash in portfolios that can meet payment obligations now. Perhaps there is money coming in – cash inflows greater than cash outflows, which can be put toward payment obligations as they come in. Or, finally, the unit may have no money coming in today, but expect money eventually: an excess of the present value of future receipts over the present value of future payments. If a lender can be convinced of the likelihood of this excess, it could serve as the basis for a loan. The anticipated future surplus would thus provide cash now. These three categories – cash on hand, cash coming in, cash in the future – Minsky memorably dubbed "hedge," "speculative," and "Ponzi," respectively (1975d, 152; also 1977c).

The names are meant to convey the relative certainty of the financing patterns, decreasing in order. Hedge finance relies on cash in hand; speculative finance requires that cash flows be sustained; Ponzi finance depends on a far-off payday. Ponzi finance is named for the Boston swindler of the 1920s, though one might look to Bernard Madoff for a more recent example. The term captures quite well the precarious position of the economic actor that must continually increase its borrowing, capitalizing its interest payments, effectively paying old lenders using the proceeds from new loans, all while hoping for a big payoff, in a future often only hazily perceived. The comparison to pyramid schemes, even without outright fraud, was a useful illustration of financial unsustainability – whether the unsustainable unit is a business or the state of California.

Ponzi finance requires continuously increasing cash support; it is unsustainable because sources of cash are not unlimited. Although much has been made of Minsky's memorable taxonomy, the three categories are nothing more than particular ways, more and less sustainable, of making position. That classification focuses on quantitative arrangements of cash flows in time. We might also consider, however, the possibility of variation in the manner by which the survival constraint is met. It is not only the amount and timing, but also the form of transaction that causes instability to arise from position-making.

Anticipating the need to make position, an economic unit need not hold cash *per se*; it has only to quickly be able to come up with cash when the need arises. Rather than holding money, that is, an actor might hold something readily sold for money, or readily hypothecated – pledged as collateral – to borrow money: Treasury bills, for example, in the post-war period. When the need arises, such an asset can readily be used to obtain cash: it's the next best thing.

The cash that buys those Treasuries, or is lent against them, must come from somewhere, and on short notice. From where? There is a source, in tranquil economic times at least: money can come from other actors, from those who *do* happen to have cash on hand. Cash that is held in reserve by some, but not needed just yet, can provide the funds to meet the more urgent needs of other debtors: "The basic raw material for the money market is the existence of pools of excess liquidity" (1967a, 53f.; also 1982c). This works, so long as there are plenty of surplus units with cash to spare and who are willing to transact in short-term funding markets. If there are enough units in surplus relative to the number in deficit, cash washes back and forth among them and markets are in general *liquid* (1975a). "In a smoothly working money market, the surpluses and deficits will be matched" (1967a, 54).

\* \* \*

In the 1960 study Minsky had constructed a theory of crisis that emphasized the spreading of an initial cash shortfall; it was a way of adding a consideration of liquidity to Schumpeter's understanding of the cycles of capitalism. In the 1965 book, with its focus on the possibility for intervention in the system of California banks, he asked after the circumstances that could make such a system vulnerable to disruption. The survival constraint defines the requirement to pay at the level of an individual institution; it is the process of position-making that moves the shortfall of a single actor to the system more generally. Seeking to fulfill a maturing commitment, an actor taps its position-making markets or instruments, borrowing from pockets of cash elsewhere in the financial system. Whether a disturbance spreads or dies out, then, depends on whether this position-making does or does not trigger further position-making:

> A financial system acts as an amplifier of depressing shocks when three consequences occur: (1) when losses of the financial system are passed on as widespread losses to the holders of financial system liabilities; (2) when the way in which financial organizations attempt to protect themselves against losses generates greater losses and defaults than would otherwise occur; and (3) when financing conditions tighten whenever income has fallen. (1965b, 126)

The crisis spreads when the debt of financial institutions comes into doubt, as their ability to pay is threatened by the shortfalls of their own customers; when position-making by some actors threatens the viability of others, propagating rather than containing the failure; and when doubt and fear render holders of cash less willing to deploy it in helping others meet their commitments. These are three ways that financial distress can spread; all can be understood as position-making problems. The inability of some actors to make position, that is, makes itself felt in the market price of negotiable claims, in cascading defaults, and in tightening credit driven by anxiety.

\* \* \*

Position-making works when the cash of surplus actors can be made available to fund deficit actors. It can be achieved using many different arrangements, all of which achieve these same ends. Pockets of money – cash pools – might be moved from surplus unit to deficit unit according to a pre-arranged contract rather than in an asset market. Innovations in such arrangements contributed to the spectacular nature of the 2008 financial crisis. For example, the typical cash need of a finance company might be to obtain the funds needed to make mortgage loans, and it might normally meet this need by issuing its own short-term debt in the commercial paper market. But it would also need a fallback to guard against the possibility that the commercial paper market could become illiquid, making it impossible for the finance company to make position by selling debt. In the early 2000s, finance companies' banks, confident of their own cash pools, and for a fee, offered liquidity puts – standing offers, with pre-agreed terms, to buy the finance company's debt (FCIC 2011, 138). The systemic consequences of such arrangements were really only understood after the crisis, when these lines of credit were tested by the need to make position.

Pockets of money in one part of the financial structure can be mobilized to fund deficits in another. These cash pools, hoards of surplus funds, disjointedly owned, can thus become linked by the contracts and practices by which actors habitually make position. Innovative bankers have provided no shortage of variations: we can understand securitization, another innovation that played a role in the 2008 crisis, as another instance. Tranching, for example, is nothing more than assigning cash to a list of hoards in sequence: first the most senior, then the next, and so on to the most junior. The Commission is at its most poetic: "Bankers often compared it to a waterfall; the holders of the senior tranches – at the top of the waterfall – were paid before the more junior tranches. And if payments came in below expectations, those at the bottom would be the first to be left high and dry" (FCIC 2011, 43).

"Hedge, speculative, Ponzi" is passable marketing for an economist, and the slogan has helped secure Minsky's distinction, but these categories are just one way of describing the ways that cash flows can become connected throughout the financial system. Structured finance offers far more intricate possibilities for arranging cash pools. As we shall see, these arrangements – standing offers to buy, sequential orders to pay, and so on – can describe the world of linked payments that Minsky observed, and which gives rise periodically to crisis.

## Economizing on reserves

With their eye on the survival constraint, anticipating the need to make position, households and businesses must try to maintain access to hoards of cash out of which they can make payment as needed. Reserves can be pledged between agents in the financial system, and new types of arrangement can easily be brought into existence by which to do so. Because such innovation responds to the needs of those looking for funding, the result is that cash is stretched ever more thinly over the course of a sustained boom. Minsky observed this phenomenon in several guises over his career, and gave it the evocative name of "layering."

As with the survival constraint that provides the motivation for layering, Minsky was certainly pointed toward it by his teacher Simons. Accepting the futility of fixing the quantity of money, Simons wrote that it "might merely serve to increase the perverse variability in the amounts of 'near-moneys' and in the degree of their general acceptability" (Simons 1948, 164). If a scarcity of one kind of money were imposed, Simons saw, it would simply spur actors to innovation, making promises to one another that could serve as close substitutes. To achieve the desired level of spending, financial innovators can invent either new kinds of money, or new ways to exchange money more quickly.

Minsky observed early in his career that this flexibility in the financial system would be used to solve the ever-present problem of position-making. The Federal Reserve might try to make borrowed money more expensive, so that businesses might resist the temptation to overextend themselves. But in a financial system that is permissive of private financial arrangements, this cannot stop actors pushing back, finding ways to make money easier to come by, so that they might more readily succumb (1963b).

Minsky had formed a picture of layering as a participant observer in the New York brokerage Garvin, Bantel and Company (1957a). He described changing institutional features of the New York money markets, in particular patterns in the usage of the Federal Funds market. The period was marked by a high and rising cost of funds, so that banks were motivated to find ways to stretch their reserves farther. "With rising interest rates the incentives to find new ways to finance operations and new substitutes for cash assets increase" (1957a, 182). The Federal Funds market allowed banks to make position by borrowing from one another, rather than from the central bank. Each bank could draw on the reserves of the other banks participating in the market, rather than only on its own limited sources of funds.

The phenomenon is not specific to the Federal Funds market. Over the course of a sustained boom, assessments of the future course of speculative activity are positive, so liquid assets, reserves, are seen as plentiful. Times are good, fortunes are rising, markets are liquid, and so there is no need to keep cash on hand. Those who do have cash, by the same argument, can readily lend it out to those who need it. As the central bank tightens the availability of cash, the willingness to pay only rises, and cash is stretched even thinner. Minsky described the effect in terms of velocity: "The financing of investment by increasing velocity increasingly takes the form of specialized institutions 'borrowing short' to 'invest long.' The growth and expansion of such financial institutions increases during a sustained boom" (1964a, 248).

We should understand "increasing velocity" as a description of *layering*: the underlying caches of the means of payment are pledged, then pledged again, then pledged again, so long as the boom proceeds. Observing the Federal Funds market, Minsky saw that layering would work fine as long as markets were working well: as long as banks are happy to lend to one another, it makes little difference if a loan of funds comes from a commercial bank or from the central bank itself. It is when the money markets tip over into instability that the difference becomes clear: layering means that more and more position-making becomes dependent on a smaller and smaller set of underlying sources of funds. It is more difficult to replace these second- and third-order sources when markets stop functioning. (It is clear that Minsky accepted velocity as a way of thinking about the degree of layering relative to the more fixed availability of higher-quality reserves, and not as a constant rate as in the quantity theory of money, which he was at pains to reject.)

This story played out over the several cycles of Minsky's career. It played out again more recently, as the managers of collateralized debt obligations found they needed to economize on cash as the securitization boom proceeded in the mid-2000s. An illustration comes, once again, from the collateralized debt obligations that were a central feature of that boom. The equity tranche of a CDO is the last to get paid, and so it is the first to take losses. An actor holding the equity tranche must therefore have cash reserves to hand. Early in the boom, CDO managers retained the equity tranches of the securitizations they had created, as a signal of their confidence in their product. Later they prized their cash more highly, and the equity tranches were sold to other holders, along with the rest of the securitization: "ACA Management, a unit of the financial guarantor ACA Capital, provides a good illustration of this trend. ACA held 100% of the equity in the CDOs it originated in 2002 and 2003, 52% and 61% of two deals it originated in 2004, between 10% and 25% of deals in 2005, and between 0% and 11% of deals in 2006" (FCIC 2011, 190).

Like CDO managers, banks too sought to allocate their reserves carefully during the boom, and indeed they are required to do so by banking regulations. They saw themselves as making scarce reserves available to support the securitization market, for a price. The price did not, in the end, prove sufficient to compensate for the risk. "[T]he biggest commercial banks and investment banks ... often touted the 'balance sheet' that they could make available to support the sale of new securities. ... Citigroup retained significant exposure to potential losses on its CDO business ... [F]ew did so as aggressively or, ultimately, with such losses" (FCIC 2011, 196). Both banks and CDO managers were pushing their efforts in layering, trying to stretch their cash as far as possible. CDO managers such as ACA worked to minimize the commitment of their resources; Citigroup sought to extract a suitable price for the allocation of its own cash. The mechanisms of securitization and the exuberant climate of the boom made it easy for them to do so.

Over the course of a boom, underlying cash reserves are pledged repeatedly as layering increases. The effects of this increase in financial complexity are not immediately visible. When funds are not too scarce, when the survival constraint does not bind too tightly for too many, a promise to pay cash is about as good as cash itself, and a promise to deliver a promise to pay cash is not too much worse (1975a). The downside, of course, shows up only when the boom comes to its end. The survival constraint begins to close in for some, who must make position and so turn to their sources of cash. But because that cash has been stretched thin over the course of the boom, the distinction between cash and a promise to pay cash becomes much sharper. Soon no interest rate is high enough to entice lenders, and the scramble for cash is on (1966b).

Minsky noticed early in his career that layering as a mechanism to economize on reserves was a widespread financial pattern. It is not a mechanical process, nor entirely predictable, nor is it even necessarily observable in real time. Rather, it is a reasonable tendency of a system in which the need to pay prompts a sense of urgency, and one that permits financial innovation, that allows a promise to stand in for final settlement, lessening that urgency. All payment systems entail the use of credit. In the complex arrangements that become possible with these conditions, it does not take much to push the system toward fragility.

*  *  *

The layering of financial commitments would contribute to the spreading of an initial financial disturbance. Minsky saw a similar strain in the financing patterns associated with California's growth. To the extent that such growth depended on borrowing from outside of the state, then any shortfall in growth would aggravate position-making efforts, sapping resources and amplifying a downturn:

> If rapid growth is financed by capital imports, and especially if debt instruments are used, payment commitments grow with the stock of outstanding indebtedness. As a result, the prospect is increased that the financial system will amplify any depressing tendencies. Because of the burden of capital imports and the way in which the growth of California depends upon the continued growth of federal expenditures in the state, the economy of California is particularly vulnerable to a slowdown or decrease in federal spending in the state. (1965c, 8)

A decade on from his observations of the Fed Funds market, Minsky found in California's situation the same underlying mechanism that he had seen there. The institutional forms were different, but the challenges would be much the same: the requirement to pay would become more burdensome by virtue of the greater stretching of the underlying means of payment. In California as in the New York money markets, that stretching was pursued to make funds available to take advantage of a boom; in both places, the risk was that increasingly layered arrangements would be increasingly liable to vanish. A binding survival constraint would trigger a rush to make position, and the layered financial structure would show its vulnerability:

> However, borrowing from Home Loan Banks, sale of local mortgages to FNMA [Fannie Mae], selling of positions in national assets such as government bonds, and borrowing from the Federal Reserve System, all of which may be needed if the local financial system is to meet its commitments due to the withdrawal of out-of-state deposits, leave behind a residue of obligations which tend to constrain the expansion

of the economy in subsequent periods. Commercial banks and savings and loan associations heavily in debt, or with "unbalanced" portfolios as a result of the flight of hot money, use the funds they receive due to their assets to repay debts and correct portfolios rather than to acquire new local loans and mortgages. That is, financial institutions, in an effort to put their "house in order," will further depress the local economy beyond that caused by the change in federal government spending. (1965b, 133; also 1966a)

Minsky trained his focus on California's financial system, a new set of observations for the same observer. The changing object of study reveals what insights come from the observer himself, what ideas constitute his maintained theory. That theory is quite well described by the survival constraint, position-making, and layering. The work of the California study was an opportunity for Minsky to further extend his analytical frame, which had grown from his dissertation work and in the study for the Commission on Money and Credit. That refinement was more durable than any particular conclusion about California; the imperative to study the financial relationships among banks within the state implied a more elaborate hierarchical structure than Minsky had previously considered. This showed the importance of position-making, of the institutional form taken by the arrangements between institutions. Minsky's financial theory was taking shape in the process.

Minsky had reached the conclusion that California's growth would come to an end, though he did not give that unsustainability the label "Ponzi" for another two years. But even if the flow of cash from out-of-state dropped, it seemed, from the perspective of 1965, that position-making was assured, that cash shortfalls could be met. Instability was a possibility, but institutions were sufficient to damp out disturbances to cash flows, and another depression was unlikely. The study offers a reassuring conclusion: "Although we cannot expect financial institutions to act as shock absorbers if a radical change in expectations takes place, it seems likely that they will not amplify the contractionary forces to the same extent as they have in the past" (1965b, 134). This viewpoint of Minsky's, however, was to be challenged by subsequent experience; the period of tranquil finance – without financial crisis – was brought to an end in the following year. His approach to economic analysis was solidified, but the facts were changing, and new questions were coming to the fore.

\* \* \*

# 4

# *The inadequacy of economics*

## Iatrogenesis

Minsky's work has achieved a certain renown, has been well received in the financial profession, and at the height of recent financial crises his name has circulated widely. Yet within the economics profession – despite his sterling credentials – Minsky's work remains relegated to the margins. He responded to this in many ways: discussing a paper by John B. Taylor, at the time just six years out from his Stanford PhD and twenty-seven years Minsky's junior, Minsky wrote: "[T]he paper serves no useful purpose aside from being a showcase for Taylor's talents … the underlying literature may be best interpreted as the products of a game played for academic advancement" (1980d, 114). One can find many such examples in Minsky's writing, and it is difficult to disagree with his assessment.

One might dismiss these jabs: every discipline has its insiders and outsiders, and the outsiders resent the privileges – academic advancement, for example – afforded to the insiders. And indeed, Minsky seemed to relish being a provocateur – he directed his pointed comments at his nominal allies with little more reserve than at his foes. There is, however, a sharper angle to Minsky's critique: "In part, the malaise of capitalist countries is iatrogenic – the disease has been induced in the patient by physicians" (1982d, 13; also 1978b; 1980d). Economic theory was making things worse.

Minsky almost certainly encountered the word *iatrogenic* in Ivan Illich's *Medical Nemesis*. Illich takes on the medical establishment, arguing that Western societies were healthier largely in spite of advances in Western medicine, not because of them, and indeed that medicine was making health worse, not better: "the damage done by medicine to the health of individuals and populations is very significant" (Illich 1976, 15). Minsky found in Illich's argument a perfect parallel to what he perceived in the economics profession. It wasn't just that economists were indulging in virtuosic but pointless displays of erudition – they were actively contributing to inflation, unemployment, and instability.

Minsky's objection was in this instance quite specific. To rein in inflation, which was on the rise again following a period of disinflation after the 1975 crisis, the Carter administration advertised a tough stance on rising prices. The attendant monetary constraint would result in unemployment and excess capacity, but this should be accepted, economists argued, as the necessary sacrifice for bringing inflation under control, and growth should be supported with other inducements for business to undertake investment. Minsky objected, however, that high interest rates would make financing more expensive while depressing demand, and therefore would increase the likelihood of a damaging financial crisis, like those of 1966, 1970, and 1974. This possibility was discounted by other economists because they were using a theory that did not really allow for financial disruptions of that kind, recent memory of that experience notwithstanding. Adherence to their discipline's methodological conventions relegating finance to a secondary status was in effect leading economists to make proposals that were adding fuel to the fire.

\* \* \*

The experience of financial instability, no longer out of childhood memory and the history of the Depression but out of his own adult experience of financial crisis, gave sharp relevance to Minsky's work. In his earlier projects, instability was a lurking possibility, and the analytical task was to use his understanding of the mechanisms of payment, and the institutions of banking, to explore that possibility. His dissertation, the 1960 and 1965 studies, and the smaller papers and projects all provided opportunities to elaborate the perspective. The Crunch of 1966, however, brought a new urgency to Minsky's work. Instability was no longer an abstract possibility to be evaluated, but an urgent reality to be addressed. The need to develop a new mode of analysis was no longer just an expansive academic adventure; it had become necessary to understand the headlines.

Minsky's (1975c) book *John Maynard Keynes* was to be a major milestone in his intellectual development. The theoretical apparatus grows out of a series of papers in the early 1970s, but much of the book is dedicated to new material defending a claim to the mantle of Keynes. Read as evidence of Minsky's own way of being an economist, the book is mostly continuous with the perspective of his earlier work, a perspective that had been expressed without substantial reference to Keynes.

The framing motivation for the 1975 book is that the insights of Keynes had been lost as his work had been incorporated into the discipline. Minsky notes the urgency of responding to the banking failures of the Depression, and it is not hard to see that he must have had in mind his own unheeded warnings around the crises of 1966, 1970, and 1974–5. "During the years of anguish between 1929 and the appearance of *The General Theory*, the dominant orthodox academic economists had little to offer in the way of politically palatable suggestions for an active public policy" (1975c, 5). Here and elsewhere, Minsky is interpreting himself as the heir to Keynes, in conflict with the orthodoxy of his day as Keynes, Minsky argues, was with the orthodoxy of his own. At times the autobiographical comes close to the surface, as when Minsky writes of his own undergraduate professor Simons:

> In the writings of the most persuasive economist in this group, Henry L. Simons of Chicago, the flaws in the American economy that led to the Great Depression were seen as mainly due to institutional weaknesses in the banking system and human errors by the authorities rather than systemic, essential characteristics of a capitalist economy. As it is always possible after the event of a crash or a crisis to impute what went wrong to some human error or institutional flaw, the Simons position is essentially irrefutable. As a result of the traditional nature of the theoretical model from which Simons argued, his policy prescriptions, though moving in the appropriate direction from the perspective of the later, Keynesian theory, were not conclusions derived from a systematic, integrated analytical formulation. ... Simons was, so to speak, dealing with symptoms rather than the causes of the then seemingly obvious flaws in capitalism. (1975c, 6)

It is probably more enlightening to read this paragraph as a summary of Minsky's own intellectual trajectory than as history of economics; Minsky is acknowledging his debt to Simons, strong in "intuition and perceptive observations," but ultimately weak in analytical foundations. Pointed in the right direction by his mentor, it had now fallen to Minsky to advance the work, and the book was to be his effort to do so. The resulting analysis would be out of the norm, as Simons's had been, but systematic. Such an analysis was needed, not least in support of intelligent policy-making. Looking back to the policy failures that created the context for the acceptance of Keynes's work, Minsky writes

> Even though Franklin Roosevelt was an activist, who wanted to do something to revive the economy, the first phalanx of economic advisors he brought to Washington to serve as house intellectuals were unable to offer him serious, systematic advice on how to go about it. Under their influence Roosevelt undertook a policy of tinkering with the dollar price of gold in an effort to raise prices – especially agricultural prices. (1975c, 6)

It is a transparent echo of Minsky's critiques of the policy-advising economists that he saw as his own opponents. As Keynes faced Roosevelt's phalanx, Minsky was to face (after 1976) a "Georgian phalanx" of advisors around US President Jimmy Carter: "The problems as defined for the administration and the policy options which are considered reflect the tunnel vision imposed by the neoclassical synthesis" (1978b, 43). In *John Maynard Keynes*, that is, Minsky was carving out an understanding of himself against the orthodoxy, not only as Keynes's intellectual heir, but indeed filling his shoes.

\* \* \*

The components of Minsky's view of an essentially financial capitalism, described in chapter 2 and theorized in chapter 3, were often delivered with some version of this message: an economic theory that does not accept finance as a first principle could not possibly address the main problem, namely that the system tends periodically to bouts of costly instability. In a way it is striking how consistently Minsky conveyed this message over the years, especially in those texts where he directly addressed the economics profession (for example, 1969c; 1972a; 1974b; 1974f; 1982d). Though economic theory was not unchanging over this period, there was little substantial movement toward incorporating the monetary, institutional features that were essential to Minsky's thought.

The difference in focus seemed to Minsky to come down to a choice between, on the one hand, studying the world, the actual institutions of a capitalist economy, and, on the other, participating in the various "games" of the economics profession, like Taylor's paper on stabilization theory, or in very similar language, "the enterprise, or game, of building large-scale econometric models" (1969c, 295). Looking back, Minsky traced the problem to formation, and suggested that the discipline should instead be taught in the context of the social sciences. "The current American way of teaching economics leads to American economists who are well trained but poorly educated," mathematically adept but unable to confront social questions (1985b, 214). He would surely have agreed with the more poetic Shackle:

> [W]e are all indoctrinated with ideals of mathematical incisive sculpture of thought, even of achieving, in however modest a degree, mathematical beauty, the surprising revelation of necessity. I am not sure that these ideals and ambitions are true for us, whose subject-matter is the ineffably mysterious, mutable and subtle nature and capacities of man. (Shackle 1988, 169)

There is little to be gained by railing against the inadequacies of the economics discipline: Minsky himself made little headway despite decades of effort, and even the crisis of 2008 has done little to address his most damning concern: the absence of any kind of recognizable financial system from economic models. Pointed and public critiques such as Ferguson's film *Inside Job*, which documents economists' iatrogenic complicity in enabling the financial conditions that led to the subprime crisis, complete with deer-in-the-headlights shots of compromised prominent academics, have had no noticeable effect on this score.

It therefore seems more promising to follow Minsky's call to pursue the broader study of society, without requiring fealty to narrow methodological constraints. His financial capitalism is a description of market society that makes an appropriately central place for finance. That perspective leads to several important avenues of thought, places in which economic theory has system-atically erred. Minsky reminds us that replicating these failures, encoding them in policy and theory, has consequences for material conditions.

The sections of this chapter that follow consider several of these points. Each takes up a theme on which Minsky differed from his colleagues in the economics profession: he focuses on cash flows over income, on nominal quantities over real, on liquidity over solvency. One might say equivalently that a payments theory of finance looks at money paid, not promised; at money transactions, not barter transactions; at a portfolio's ability to yield money, not its notional market value. I return to these themes in chapter 7, where I look at the relationship of Minsky's work to that of Keynes, and its position within the economics discipline today.

## Cash flow over income

Minsky resolutely took a banker's view of the world. He saw payment as the essential mechanism of capitalism, and built a theory around the modalities of payment: the urgency created by the survival constraint, the search set in motion by position-making, the strained complexity created by the layering of contracts. Each of these is a banking concept that need not remain tied to the institutions and instruments of banking as such; if every economic actor is thought of as a bank, these become more general descriptions of the basic behavioral patterns of financial capitalism.

This vision is the starting point for Minsky's work, on which he builds a theory of finance to understand investment and the business cycle. But the perspective is alien to economics, which takes payment as a mechanical operation of no further interest. This underlying difference in viewpoint shows up in several forms.

The first form is Minsky's choice to focus on *cash flow over income*. The difference is familiar from accounting; it is the same as that between accounting on an accrual basis, where transactions are recorded at the moment they are agreed, and on a cash basis, where transactions are recorded at the moment they are settled in money. Economics takes the former as substantive, calling it income; it ignores the latter, which we call cash flow. It is a difference in perspective – two sets of ideas about the same circumstances. The income view treats the agreement to transact as the substantive event; the cash-flow view treats settlement in cash as the substantive event.

In terms of Minsky's theory, a cash flow is the act of payment; income is a promise of payment. The gap between the two concepts has to do precisely with the possibility that payment may not be made as promised. If the fulfillment of a promise is taken to be certain, then the promise is as good as payment itself. The extent to which the creditors to any particular borrower suppose that its promises are likely to be fulfilled is a measure of its creditworthiness. The extent to which creditors in general suppose that the promises of borrowers in general will be made as promised is a measure of the overall level of optimism, exuberance, or delusion.

* * *

Minsky brought his priors – his maintained theory – to the task of interpreting Keynes. That vision, the payments view of capitalism which places finance at its center, owes more to Schumpeter and to Simons than it does to Keynes. Minsky came to the book as an active interpreter, with his priors as the basis for the creation of an interpretation. The history that had unfolded over his two decades as an economist seemed to confirm the validity of his view; Keynes's work could provide additions to the maintained theory and could serve as a disciplinary beachhead from which to expand the attack on economics. One of the major efforts of *John Maynard Keynes* would thus be to render Keynes's ideas in Minsky's language of cash flows:

> The conclusion to our argument is that the missing step in the standard Keynesian theory was the explicit consideration of capitalist finance within a cyclical and speculative context. Once capitalist finance is introduced and the development of cash flows (as stated in the inter-related balance sheets) during the various states of the economy is explicitly examined, then the full power of the revolutionary insights and the alternative frame of analysis that Keynes developed becomes evident. (1975c, 129)

The 1965 book had been an opportunity to study the financial system of California. Minsky applied a payments view of financial capitalism to develop a view as to the patterns and stability of such a system. A decade later, his focus was not on California but on the work of Keynes. The underlying theory of financial capitalism was still very much in evidence. In outlining his interpretation of Keynes, Minsky reminds us of position-making and the layering of cash commitments as potential sources of instability:

> [I]n a boom the ingenuity of bankers is directed at turning every possible source of temporarily idle cash into a source of financing for either real operations or financial position making. The tendency therefore is to generate endogenously a structure of cash-payment commitments which embodies an ever-closer articulation of cash payment and receipts, and in which an ever-larger portion of units is forced to refinance debts when due. Thus units become ever more dependent upon the normal functioning of financial as well as product and factor markets. A sharp change occurs when position making

by refinancing breaks down ... In these circumstances, the pace of investment can, and does, quickly slow down. (1975c, 143)

These rehearsals of his theory of financial capitalism go alongside more direct interpretations of Keynes. In thinking about unemployment – one of the central questions that *The General Theory* had addressed – Minsky brings familiar principles to bear: owners of capital are money-in-money-out devices, like banks, and their capital assets are sources of cash flows. Keynes's understanding of aggregate demand, that is, becomes for Minsky a source of cash inflows for the owners of the capital stock; the level of employment has to do with the sufficiency of these inflows or quasi-rents:

> If we assume fixed proportions in production, then the amount of capital services entrepreneurs wish to use also determines the amount of labor they wish to employ. Whereas capital services not used today will be available some other day, labor services not used are lost forever. Cyclical unemployment is more due to the total demand being insufficient to yield large enough quasi-rents [than] it is due to wage income not meeting some standard. (1975c, 138)

Unemployment, that is, is due to a poorly functioning economy, not to workers' unwillingness to work at the wages available. The argument is reminiscent of Minsky's work on poverty. Then he had noted that shifts in aggregate demand would be needed to bring people out of unemployment; here he follows Keynes and elaborates the role of the owners of capital. That elaboration, as always, involves understanding entrepreneurs, like workers, as balancing cash flows.

\* \* \*

Minsky's layering, the mechanisms of economizing on reserves, serving to stretch liquidity over the course of a boom, is invisible if the difference between cash flow and income is elided. Economizing on reserves is nothing more than making promises to pay money in lieu of actually paying money. If promises are as good as payment, there need not be any limit to this stretching. It is a characteristic both of a boom and of economic theory that promises are taken at face value. Without the focus on the survival constraint, on the moment of payment, present in Minsky's theory and absent in economics, it is hard to perceive the systemic erosion of credit that is characteristic of an aging boom. When it is finally revealed, it comes as a surprise if one sees only income and not cash flow.

The difference in perspective means that the national-accounts statistics that are available for quantitative research do not measure the right thing. They are based on the national income identity, a categorization of transactions that constitute sources of income (wages, profits, dividends) and uses of income (consumption, government spending, investment). Minsky made some attempts to use available data to quantify cash flows as distinct from income, and saw a more thorough effort as necessary for understanding financial instability. This would combine measurements of cash flows relating to income with those relating to portfolio adjustments. "In particular the changing relations between cash receipts and payment obligations and between payment obligations and the margins of safety need [to] be understood" (1980a, 237; also 1964b).

Morris Copeland's work to develop a system of national "money-flows" accounts were an effort in this direction (Copeland 1952). (I cannot find any evidence that Minsky was aware of Copeland's work, though surely he would have found it sympathetic.) Copeland's innovation was precisely to focus on cash flows where the GDP accounts focus on income. The central questions in this view are synonymous with Minsky's: what payments are made, and what is the source of money for those payments? Copeland, however, sought to factor out those purely financial, money-for-money transactions that constitute the flux of financing activity; surely Minsky would have wanted these included as a window on the layering of payment commitments. Copeland's prototype became a reality in compromised form as the US Flow of Funds accounts, now called the Financial Accounts, and by their theoretical principles neither Copeland nor Minsky would be satisfied.

Minsky himself was not entirely consistent in distinguishing cash flows and income. He viewed profits as the economic flow that would eventually compensate successful enterprises for their efforts, thus *validating*, confirming that debt was wisely undertaken for this purpose. (I return to validation later.) "Profits are critical in a capitalist economy because they are a cash flow which enables business to validate debt *and* because anticipated profits are the lure that induces current and future investment. It is anticipated profits which enable business to issue debts to finance investment and positions in capital assets" (1980a, 226). Here Minsky goes wrong. Profits are income, not cash flow; only when profits are paid as promised are they a source of positive cash flow and a lure for investment. It is a characteristic of good economic times that there is no difficulty realizing paper gains in money, and so the elision is without consequence; it is in the following bust that it becomes difficult to actually get paid.

## Nominal over real

Minsky's perspective shows up also in a second point of difference from the economics orthodoxy: *nominal over real*. Economic theory customarily reckons values in terms of goods – considered to be "real" values – rather than in terms of money. At its simplest, this is explained as filtering out the effect of changing prices from the effect of changing patterns of consumption and production. Real GDP, for example, is meant to convey something about the changing quantity of stuff produced by a society, separately from changes in the price of that stuff. There is already a contradiction here, because even "real" GDP is expressed in money terms – how else could the entire product of an economic unit be expressed as a single number?

This preference for "real" quantities over nominal has another manifestation, in the modeling of behavioral preferences. Minsky cites Hahn in discussing the so-called axiom of reals: "the objectives of agents that determine their actions and plans do not depend on any nominal magnitudes. Agents care only about 'real' things, such as goods (properly dated and distinguished by states of nature), leisure and effort" (Hahn 1983; cited in Minsky 1984c, 454). Those who, like Minsky, object to this axiom are dismissed as suffering from "money illusion": one thinks about money prices only as the consequence of a delusion about the nature of value.

It is in such a context, a world in which only goods and services matter and money is just a source of illusions, that the Walrasian model of markets is set. The microeconomic framework that has served as the basis of economic theory since the Marginal Revolution of the late nineteenth century is based on an equality between supply and demand for goods in an abstract market. It is, as Minsky observed, an elaboration of a barter paradigm, one in which goods are traded directly for other goods. Money, in such a world, enters only as a way to separate the moment of purchase from the moment of sale, a major increase in convenience – a reduction in transaction costs – but not a source of economic phenomena in its own right: money is a counter, the denominator for prices, a numeraire, but not more than that (1975c; 1983e; 1985d).

\* \* \*

In sorting out his relationship to Keynes, Minsky had to reconcile the deep insights he saw in Keynes's work with the shortcomings he was seeking to correct. On the one hand *The General Theory* offered a resonant channel by which Minsky's argument could be amplified as it had not been in its previous forms; on the other hand Keynes's work had to have been both imperfectly expressed, and misleadingly interpreted, to give Minsky occasion to correct it. Keynes's reversion to a world of barter, of the trade of goods for goods, seemed to run against his focus on the role of money as a determinant of demand, and was one of the entry points for Minsky:

> Why the financial aspects were left essentially implicit, why they were subject to allusion rather than detailed argumentation in *The General Theory*, I do not know. Perhaps ... Keynes was like a snake shedding his skin as he was writing *The General Theory*, and the book was written when the old skin – the classical view – was not fully off. Thus Keynes in *The General Theory* did not emerge with a full-blown cyclical and financial analysis and a critique of capitalism. Enough of the barter paradigm remained in his thinking so that he did not make the final step to an analysis of the capitalist process that is fully rooted in "the City" and "Wall Street." (1975c, 129)

This critique, leveled here at Keynes and later at other interpreters of Keynes, is an important one for Minsky. The content of the critique is that simplification to a world of barter suppresses the possibility of credit. If goods are understood to be paid for essentially with goods, it is very hard to make a place for the role of loans of money. The barter abstraction supposes that such loans are unproblematic; yet the financial instability that motivated Minsky – as it motivated Keynes – makes little sense under such assumptions.

* * *

To suppose that there is a more "real," less illusory reality in which money disappears and only other things remain is tantamount to a negation of the survival constraint. In a barter system, the question is not whether one can pay, but whether one possesses something of value. The market produces a set of prices at which exchange proceeds. Even if toy versions of money and debt are allowed in, prices and payments are assumed to follow mechanically – there is no separate idea of payment. But the survival constraint says, in contrast, that when the payment comes due, it must be made in money. Debts are, really, denominated in money, and so the question of whether or not one can pay is a nominal question. A payments theory of finance makes sense only in a nominal world.

The distinction between payment in money and an underlying physical asset illustrates the importance of this distinction. One might consider the position of the lender in a defaulted mortgage in the 2008 crisis. The logic of a mortgage is that the lender can take possession of the collateral, the house, to compensate for their losses if the borrower is unable to pay. In a systemic crisis, however, the market value of the collateral, the market price of the house, will have fallen precipitously – the proceeds from selling it will not make up for the losses on the loan. Thus the collateral does not easily wipe away the loan: the bank's own position-making needs require money, not real estate, and selling the house for money is likely to be problematic. The barter paradigm can recognize the change in price only as a symptom of demand falling relative to supply, not as a symptom of dysfunctional markets, and so there is no way to connect the systemic financial fragility around lending to the fall in prices.

Minsky sees it from the bankers' point of view: "[B]ankers always live in a 'nominal' world" (1985c, 14), or more colorfully, "As consumers, bankers may choose among clarets and hocks, but as bankers they are concerned about cash flows and the nominal value of assets" (1984c, 454; also 1986g). Indeed, to give finance a central role requires that the distinction be discarded. "[T]here is no division between what orthodox theorists call 'the real' and 'the nominal'" (1989c, 49). Bankers live in a nominal world; everyone is a banker; so everyone lives in a nominal world; or more simply: the world is nominal.

For Minsky, then, it is those who cling to the barter paradigm, the Walrasian market, who are trucking in illusions. Buyers must obtain the means of payment in order to settle their debts, and the barter paradigm supposes that this is always possible in a transparent way. But this is starkly in contrast to the fact that the financial system clearly serves as a source of instability. The surest thing about financial capitalism is the survival constraint, that payment must be made in nominal terms, in money.

But should one not then proceed to pin down precisely what money is? This is the approach, in one way or another, of much monetary thought. The gold standard, for example, supposes that gold is real money and that any value that credit might have, that paper money might have, derives from the fact that it is in some way a promise to pay gold. Attempts to measure and control a quantity of money similarly require one to specify which quantity is being controlled, which leads to a sense that there is credit with varying degrees of "moneyness," and to measurements of the different things that have this property. Economics has instead tried to add bank money as an afterthought to a barter world (1989c): even if the underlying exchange is based on what is "real," one cannot deny that money exists, so it is introduced into theory at a late stage, with a relatively minor role to play.

I have followed Minsky in taking another direction. "'[M]oney means different things in different contexts" (1967a, 34). Rather than defining money and saying that payment is recognizable as the transfer of money, we have instead started with payment, which is the action that completes a transaction in a market economy. There is a whiff of circularity here: the survival constraint is the requirement to pay money, and money is what is used to satisfy the survival constraint. It is indeed circular: money is an inside phenomenon; it has no meaning outside of the bounds of the economic system. "Money ... is a product of financing activity; it is endogenous to the economy. When a unit holds money, it has title to a liability on a bank's balance sheet; this liability, together with other liabilities, finance the bank's position" (1984b, 31; also 1982c). A theory of finance that places payment at the center, as Minsky did, must take money as an irreducible concept inherently tied to the role that it plays in payment.

## Liquidity over solvency

A third version of Minsky's orientation toward payment is an emphasis on *liquidity over solvency*. An economic actor is solvent if its assets are greater than its liabilities; if the value of what it owns is greater than the value of what it owes; if its net worth is positive. Solvency is the answer to the question posed by a firm's balance sheet, which imagines that, on a given date, the business is liquidated, all its assets sold on the market, the proceeds going to pay off its liabilities. If there are funds left over, the firm is solvent; if not, it is insolvent.

Liquidity is the trickier of the two terms, because of the variety of ways the word has been used; I shall have a great deal more to say about the subject in the next chapter. Speaking about the situation of an economic actor, a household, business, or government, a first characterization is that an actor is liquid if it is in a position to force a unit of cash flow in its favor. Such a definition is oriented toward the survival constraint – an actor is liquid precisely if it can pay its debts when they come due. The definition is also consistent with position-making – the more liquid the actor, the easier its position-making task. It is, finally, consistent with the idea of economizing on reserves – if liquidity is not prized, then those who are liquid will feel no compunction about taking on new cash commitments.

In the context of financial capitalism, liquidity is the ability to get cash from one's portfolio; solvency is the portfolio's value on the market. It is liquidity that is tested by the survival constraint – one can make payment when due if and only if one can come up with the means of payment as needed, thus if one is liquid. Solvency, by this token, is at one level of remove from this question. If an actor is solvent, the logic goes, then it can sell assets to cover its obligations, and will come up positive. But this logic skips a step: it assumes that the assets can indeed be sold when needed. If an actor sells an asset to pay its debts, it is by definition trying to make position. It can raise cash in this way only if someone else has cash and is willing to buy the asset; that is, if there is someone else who is liquid. Solvency is not enough: a solvent actor can make payment only if liquidity is assumed. In some circumstances the assumption is unproblematic: if lenders have few doubts about borrowers, and if prices are not changing too quickly, then borrowers can raise cash if and only if they are solvent. But for Minsky this is precisely the point: the moments of interest, costly and disruptive financial crises, are exactly those at which the assumption fails.

Moreover, one can quite easily be liquid but not solvent. The problem with borrowers that are stringing along with Ponzi finance – with ever-increasing indebtedness, borrowing even to cover interest payments – is that they are in fact liquid. As long as lenders are willing to put up cash, they are able to make their payments. A reasonable valuation of the balance sheet of such a borrower would make them insolvent as the likelihood of the bonanza, the big payday in the distant future, is properly discounted. Prior to the 2008 crisis, so-called Option ARMs were based on such Ponzi finance: borrowers who could not make their payments would *automatically* be lent the difference (FCIC 2011). Insolvency need not be an obstacle to borrowing, and therefore an insolvent actor need not be illiquid.

Likewise, one can be solvent but not liquid. In early March of 2008, the US Securities and Exchange Commission (SEC) was attending to capital levels at Bear Stearns and found that the investment bank was solvent, that there was no reason for worry. It was the firm's sudden inability to come up with cash that brought it down:

> Hayman Capital Partners ... had decided to close out a relatively small $5 million subprime derivative position with Goldman Sachs. Bear Stearns offered the best bid, so Hayman expected to assign its position to Bear, which would then become Goldman's counterparty in the derivative. Hayman notified Goldman by a routine email on Tuesday, March 11, at 4:06 P.M. The reply 41 minutes later was unexpected: "GS does not consent to this trade."
>
> That startled Kyle Bass, Hayman's managing partner. He told the FCIC he could not recall any counterparty rejecting a routine novation. Pressed for an explanation, Goldman the next morning offered no details: "Our trading desk would prefer to stay facing Hayman. We do not want to face Bear." Adding to the mystery, 16 minutes later Goldman agreed to accept Bear Ste[a]rns as the counterparty after all. But the damage was done. The news hit the street that Goldman had refused a routine transaction with one of the other big five investment banks. The message: don't rely on Bear Stearns. (FCIC 2011, 287f.)

Goldman did not believe Bear Stearns could not make position; Bear was out of business within days, its capital cushion – its solvency – notwithstanding. It is the survival constraint that matters, and that is a question of liquidity. Solvency, leverage, and capital are helpful only to the extent that they are ways to talk about liquidity.

Many scholars of Minsky have not taken fully on board his focus on liquidity over solvency. Wray (2016), for example, sees the 2008 crisis as being principally about excessive borrowing, about the amount of outstanding liabilities relative to assets, and thus primarily a question of solvency. The underlying problem, in this view, is excessive borrowing on the part of the financial sector. "[W]hat was particularly unusual, and had long been ignored, was the unprecedented rise of financial sector indebtedness, which reached 125 percent of GDP. ... In truth, it was not simply a liquidity crisis but also a solvency crisis brought on by risky and in many cases fraudulent practices" (Wray 2016, 154). Such a view bears little relationship to Minsky's. "As one New York Fed official wrote to colleagues in July, 'Balance-sheet capital isn't too relevant if you're suffering a massive run.' If there is a run, and a firm can only get fire-sale prices for assets, even large amounts of capital can disappear almost overnight" (FCIC 2011, 324).

Minsky's theoretical emphasis on liquidity over solvency is absolute in that the central insights that makes his work distinctive, from the survival constraint to the financial instability hypothesis, and the mechanisms surrounding them, all key off of the moment of payment. Liquidity determines what happens at this moment; solvency can enter only as a factor in determining liquidity, for example when asset-price falls reduce the value of a portfolio and trigger a margin call. This is not to say that there is nothing to be said about solvency, but only that when we are following Minsky, what is always at question is payment, and therefore liquidity.

* * *

To solidify the theoretical connection to the work of Keynes that was the main objective of the 1975 book, the determination of the pace of investment had to be developed more carefully – where in 1960 Minsky could reckon in terms of instability from an unspecified source, and in 1965 he could simply point to the risk of a withdrawal of government spending in California, the more systematic attempt in 1975 required a more general analysis of investment. The resulting theory, which he advances in *John Maynard Keynes*, is expressed in language that is quite different from what he had put out before. The theory, however, is a continuous development from what Minsky had advanced earlier, and at points is clearly recognizable as such.

The effort to render Minsky's own theory as the lost theory of Keynes, however, introduced some interference, and what is left is stranded in a middle ground. Here I discuss this tension in terms of the relationship between liquidity, which Minsky returns to page after page, and solvency, present only by virtue of its complete absence from the book. Minsky's theory of investment, unsurprisingly from the point of view of the present volume, understands capital assets – that is, physical capital – primarily as a source of cash flows. Everyone is a bank, a money-in-money-out device, and physical capital, the means of production, serves primarily to generate cash flows for its owners. Ownership entails also some holding costs, likewise understood as cash commitments. Capital assets thus find their place on the balance sheet, along with financial claims:

> An ultimate reality in a capitalist economy is the set of interrelated balance sheets among the various units. Items in the balance sheets set up cash flows. Cash flows are the result of (1) the income-producing system, which includes wages, taxes, and nonfinancial corporate gross profits after taxes, (2) the financial structure, which is composed of ...

interest, dividends, rents, and repayments on loans, and (3) ... dealing
or trading in capital assets and financial instruments. For all except
dividends, the cash flows determined by the financial structure are
contractual commitments. (1975c, 118)

It is a world of balance sheets, but the actual balance between
assets and liabilities – that is, equity or net worth, thus solvency –
is rarely operative for Minsky. Balance sheets serve as containers
for assets and liabilities, whose importance is the cash flows they
generate, very much in line with Minsky's work in the Commission
on Money and Credit study, for example. With this conception of
even physical capital assets as essentially financial, Minsky diverges
from prior interpretations of Keynes. Those attempts have no survival
constraint, no sense in which the financed investment will need to
generate the cash flows to meet cash commitments on the borrowing.
They are therefore unable to account for financing problems.

This shows up, for example, in Minsky's discussion of the
investment-equals-savings (IS) curve. That relationship, still familiar
to students, proposes a direct connection between financing conditions and output: a higher interest rate makes financed investment
more costly and thus less attractive. For Minsky, the connection
goes instead through the cash flows that the investment is expected
to generate: rising interest rates increase the cost of meeting the
commitments necessitated by investment relative to the cash yields
of that investment. Investment therefore has the form of a financial
portfolio allocation decision.

The returns $q$ are the returns to enterprise. The proportion of the
returns committed by liabilities $c$ and the proportion of assets owned
that yield a return in the form of liquidity $l$ are due to speculative
decisions. Investment is the production allocation which increases
the $q$ yielding assets in an economy; the investing firm acquires these
assets by putting out its liabilities, which increases the $c$ it is committed
to pay, or by decreasing its $l$ assets. A decision to invest is a decision to
emit liabilities or decrease liquidity: the cash received in exchange for
commitments $c$ is the currency used to pay for the investment. (1975c,
89)

During a boom, owners of capital seek out more expensive sources
of liquidity as it becomes more scarce: high returns on their capital
investments mean that the survival constraint recedes as a concern.
Entrepreneurs thus take on more burdensome cash commitments as
the boom proceeds. As the extent of untapped cash pools diminishes,

the cost of accessing that cash can overtake the cash yields generated by the investment:

> As the CC's rise relative to the Q's, the gross profits after taxes and after the cash commitment due to liabilities will begin to grow less rapidly than the pace of investment and of debt. As lenders and borrowers seek new ways to finance investment, borrowers increasingly, on the margin, will tap sources of funds that value liquidity ever more highly – that is, contract terms on debts will rise. This implies that short-run cash needs due to debts can out-run the cash being generated by the Q's. This is due mainly to the short-term nature of many boom debts, which require the repayment of principal at a faster pace than the cash generated by the underlying operation permits. Units which use this type of debt need to refinance their debt as contracts fall due. (1975c, 114)

It is a theory of investment that puts borrowers' cash commitments at the center. Minsky's language takes on a new shape as he builds out the connection to Keynes, but the conclusion offers little surprise. The risk is a crisis brought on when entrepreneurs' survival constraints finally begin to bind. When sources of cash have been exhausted, position-making eventually becomes impossible, and financial disruptions follow.

> [T]here are two sets of prices and two sets of transactions. One set of prices and transactions deals with the production and distribution of current output. ... The other set of prices and transactions deals with capital assets and financial instruments. For the economy to function normally the two sets of prices must be properly aligned because investment, a part of current output, becomes a capital asset once it is produced and at work. Investment goods will not be produced and financed unless it is expected that the price of the finished product will exceed, by a large enough margin of safety to placate the fears of the unknown future, the cost of the investment good. If the prices of capital assets and financial instruments are high relative to current output, then an investment boom and inflation are likely to result; if capital asset and financial instrument prices are low relative to current output prices, then investment will be sluggish. A recession is likely to occur. (1977d, 26)

\* \* \*

# 5

# *Making the market*

## Position-making and liquidity

The most spectacular failures of the 2008 crisis were precipitated by payment difficulties. In March of that year, the investment bank Bear Stearns was forced to sell to JPMorgan Chase when it could not meet margin calls in repo and derivatives markets. Lehman Brothers filed for bankruptcy protection on September 15 in the face of increasing demands from its repo bank, also JPMorgan Chase. "They just wanted the cash," said Lehman treasurer Paolo Tonucci later (FCIC 2011, 333). AIG received emergency funding the next day; it needed cash to cover its maturing commercial paper and repo positions, while being asked to post more collateral on CDS and being able to ask less collateral in its securities lending business. The three businesses faced complex problems, but the reason that they failed when they did was that they could not make position.

Those moments were only the most visible examples of a pattern that is faced in some way by all economic actors at all times. The requirement to pay at the promised time, the survival constraint, creates the need for position-making. In doing so, we have already seen the key role for cash pools, what Minsky sometimes labeled "cash kickers," in giving economic units the capacity to make payment when due. Such pockets of money are mobilized by participants in the financial system as they scramble to meet their payment commitments. "Finance," said Hawtrey (1919, 207), is "the art of providing the means of payment." How does the financial system, the set of linked usages that connect cash pools to one another, provide the means of payment to those who need it? To a great extent this is accomplished by the activities of securities dealers, who form the subject of this chapter.

How do dealers make it easier for others to make position? Jack Treynor (1987) provides a simple analysis. A dealer, in Treynor's model, is an economic actor that makes a business of buying when its customers wish to sell, and selling when its customers wish to buy. To do this, the dealer sets a price at which it will buy and a higher price at which it will sell, and communicates to its customers these buy and sell – bid and ask – prices. Treynor's model was stated in terms of securities markets but is by no means limited to such markets. "As is true of much of economics, the real world institutions often do not fit into the abstract classes of theory" (1967a, 34f.). Treynor's is a theory of market-making that finds clean expression in the language of finance, but which describes much more general behavior in a market economy.

By making markets, dealers make it easier for their customers to make position because dealers offer to trade quickly, at an announced price. The actor who needs cash in a hurry can sell an asset to a dealer. *Liquidity* is a name for this service. Liquidity is a characteristic of the particular market in which the dealer is transacting. It is this ease of transacting that dealers provide to their customers, whether they are buying or selling. Such ease can be recognized when transactions can be completed quickly, in size, and without moving the price. When the market for a particular instrument is liquid, that instrument is more suitable for position-making.

Liquidity can also be thought of as a characteristic of an economic actor, as I did when distinguishing it from solvency in chapter 4. There I said that an actor is liquid when it can readily force a unit of cash flow in its favor. The two usages of the word are consistent: if an actor possesses assets that trade in liquid markets, then these can readily be sold to dealers for cash. Note well, however, that the liquidity of a market is a consequence of the activity of market-makers; when they stop that activity, markets become illiquid, and those who were counting on being able to sell into those markets likewise become illiquid.

Market-making is the service of liquidity provision, rendered by dealers for a price. The price is visible in the difference – the spread – between the dealer's buy and sell prices: a dealer buys from one customer, turns around and sells, at a higher price, to another. The spread is thus a source of profit for the dealer, and at the same time an expense for its customers. This motivates the way that dealers set prices: a dealer must set its prices competitively enough that its customers wish to transact; dealers compete with one another to offer the most attractive terms by pushing their bids up and their asks down, narrowing the spread and thus reducing their profits.

To see how this can happen, Treynor looks at what dealers must do in order to continue providing liquidity. When a customer wishes to sell a security, the dealer buys it with cash, adding to its inventory of securities. If many customers wish to sell the same security, the dealer may find its inventory growing larger than it would like, and so lower its ask price, offering worse terms to discourage future sellers, and lower also its bid price, offering better terms to encourage future buyers. Both changes help it reduce its now-excessive inventory. Likewise a run of purchases by customers may leave a dealer with low inventory, and the dealer can raise its bid and ask prices, encouraging sellers and discouraging buyers, to replenish its supplies (Treynor 1987; Harris 2003).

Liquidity, that is, is not an inherent quality of a security, a market, or an actor. It is a transient condition of markets, conditional on dealers' inventory adjustments. When there are plenty of buyers and plenty of sellers, small changes in a dealer's bid and ask prices will bring in many transactors, inventory adjusts easily, and in general, position-making is unproblematic. But as Bear, Lehman, and AIG discovered, this state of affairs cannot be assumed.

* * *

*John Maynard Keynes* was anomalous, among Minsky's projects, in its degree of remove from the events of the financial world, focusing instead on the text of Keynes. But the Franklin National crisis of 1974–5 would reorient Minsky's attention toward the news. The subsequent years would provide further opportunities for him to elaborate his underlying financial theory in response to the changing circumstances. Over the sections of this chapter, we follow Minsky's work on the changing role of the United States in the international monetary system, developed in a series of articles, many in non-academic publications and mostly published between 1977 and 1985. A major theme is the re-emergence of financial crisis as a pattern:

> The first time the viability of the liability structure was seriously threatened in the postwar era was in 1966. At that time, the Federal

Reserve System intervened to protect banks, savings and loan associations, and mutual savings banks. The Federal Reserve validated the debt structure. Thus, after a slight pause, the expansion of debt-financed asset acquisition resumed. The period of 1966–1970 ... culminated in the Penn-Central crisis in the commercial paper market. Once again, the Federal Reserve intervened to halt the liquidation of debt. Once again, after a slight pause, the expansion of the economy continued. At this writing (June, 1974) another embryonic financial crisis is emerging in the plight of the Franklin National Bank. ... [W]e may well go through another cycle or two of accelerating inflation as the Federal Reserve floats off a debt structure that is crisis-prone. (1974d, 33f.)

That "embryonic" crisis would grow to significant proportions. The Fed's eventual intervention in support of Franklin National demonstrated that that domestic institution now had responsibilities beyond the borders of the US. The centrality of the dollar to the global financial system meant that international disruptions could affect domestic banks. Minsky's analytical frame once again had to be adapted to changing circumstances. His answer – as ever – was to understand the US as a bank, matching cash in- and outflows. The California banking volume had been an early foray into the balance-of-payments questions that come up around cross-border payments. In that case, "cross-border" meant payments between California and the rest of the United States, and the conclusion had been that California was relying on increasing debt to sustain its economic activity. Now the same approach took the US as the accounting unit. Minsky's explanation has a familiar ring to it:

> To understand how the American economy is affected by its international posture and how policy can affect that posture, it is necessary to treat the American economy as if it was a bank. A bank is a highly levered organization whose assets are almost exclusively financial. These financial assets consist of loans and various securities. The loans set up dated, or contingent, "cash flows" to the bank, and the securities can be used to generate cash by being sold in markets in which there are always customers ready and able to buy. ... A bank is vulnerable to losing deposits which, for a loss of cash, if carried far enough, will make it impossible for the bank to fulfill its obligations. (1978c; 1990a)

The United States is an accounting unit, and so – as always in Minsky's financial capitalism – the problem it faces is the problem faced by a bank, namely the meeting of its payment commitments with its sources of cash. The US is even more like a bank in that it was issuing short-term, liquid liabilities to finance the holding of longer-term, less liquid assets. Kindleberger, Despres, and Salant (1966), writing as the strains in the international monetary system were coming into view but before the system had begun to unravel, had taken much the same perspective: the US was providing the services of liquidity transformation to the rest of the world, allowing the financing of capital assets.

A bank, like any actor, is financially viable if it can meet its survival constraint; if it can fulfill its cash commitments when needed. An entity whose balance sheet is characterized by liquidity transformation, one whose liabilities create short-term commitments and whose assets provide only long-term sources of funds, is most particularly subject to the survival constraint: one could say that it specializes in being able to generate cash when needed, and charges a premium – in the form, for example, of an interest-rate differential – as the price of doing so.

The US can be thought of as a bank, but it is a bank as an accounting unit; the actual banking business is undertaken by specific actors within that unit. The 1974–5 crisis was centered on the offshore banking business of US banks, with Franklin National Bank at the epicenter. Franklin had grown from domestic to international operations from the mid-1960s, and had financed itself in the Eurodollar market, the market for offshore dollars – US deposits traded in Europe (and elsewhere) and thus outside of the purview of the US Federal Reserve (Wolfson 1986). (The currency called the euro, whose existence gave rise to the euro–dollar exchange rate, came into existence in 1999 and introduced this small lexical ambiguity. Eurodollars are international dollars and predate the euro by decades. I will call them by the more descriptive name "offshore dollars," which is also more inclusive as the markets are not only in Europe.)

Franklin National came under pressure in May 1974. It was unable to refinance in the offshore dollar market, and became unable to meet its cash commitments. Franklin's situation was extreme, but not unique, and the panic encompassed other US banks as well. Franklin received significant support from the Federal Reserve before ultimately failing in October of that year. Minsky tried to take on board the institutional implications. Writing in *Society*:

> The failure of Franklin National was triggered by a run on its London branch and Wall Street operations after losses in its foreign exchange operations were disclosed. When Franklin National was finally closed, some $1.7 [billion] of its $3.6 billion in assets were supported by

Federal Reserve loans. As a result of this massive infusion of funds by the Federal Reserve, all the deposit liabilities of Franklin National Bank, including certificates of deposit at the overseas branch, were validated. ... [T]he Federal Reserve was in effect making every dollar of deposits at an overseas branch of a U.S. chartered bank the equivalent of a deposit in a U.S. bank. Thus in 1974 The Federal Reserve abdicated its responsibility for controlling the growth of the U.S. money supply. (1977d, 28)

The importance reaches well beyond Franklin National. When a bank struggles to make position, it needs a source of refinance. The Federal Reserve provided such support to Franklin National because the bank's early failure would have triggered further failures among US banks. But by doing so, the central bank was accepting the offshore dollar liabilities of US banks as true dollars – an international extension of the US money markets, backed by the Federal Reserve.

\* \* \*

## Dealing and initiative

"Buy low, sell high" is the source of profit for dealers, as for all enterprise; what distinguishes them is that dealers transact, not when they wish to do so, but when their customers wish to do so – that is, on their customers' initiative. To make a profit as a market-maker requires the patience to wait for customers, but also the readiness to act when a customer finally arrives. Dealer profit derives from the bid–ask spread, the difference between the dealer's buy price and its sell price. When competition among dealers makes this spread small, as is the norm in many financial markets, it is only by completing many trades, on both sides of the market, that dealers can hope to turn a profit. Dealers can try to attract customers by adjusting prices, but in the end the dealer must be patient: the trade happens on the customer's initiative.

A dealer sets its prices and waits for customers; its customers watch the prices and decide when to transact. A market-maker must be ready to transact, and so it is obliged to maintain an inventory, both of securities, ready to be sold, and of money, ready to buy. If the dealer wishes to allow its customers to trade more quickly, or in larger volume – thereby providing more liquidity – the inventory must be correspondingly larger. But such inventory is costly – funds held idle, or tied up in securities held idle, could be put to other profitable uses elsewhere. That inventories are costly to dealers is reason to minimize them. So inventories must be large enough to facilitate trade, but small enough to ensure dealer profits.

The value to transactors of a liquid market is that it makes it possible for them to act on their own *initiative*. Minsky's understanding of the role of initiative for financial intermediaries is signaled, in an offhand way, in his early observations of the New York money market (1957a). He noted there the role that repo transactions with the Federal Reserve had come to play in the financing needs of bond dealers. Since those repo transactions normally came on the initiative of the central bank, however, they could not be counted on for position-making. But Minsky noted an informative disruption to this pattern, when in June 1956 the Fed offered to undertake repo transactions with dealers on the dealers' initiative. The Fed responded to a market disruption, that is, by giving the initiative to the dealers: the central bank offered to trade when they wished, making itself into a dealer.

The idea of initiative has not received much treatment among economists. It is an act of choice, or perhaps more accurately the capacity to choose. But it is choice set in time: it is not selection from a fixed set of known alternatives, as in the utility-maximization problem of microeconomics. Initiative is rather "an uncaused cause," the capacity to set events in motion, to begin a series of events whose full course may not be known. Any such choice implies also that other possibilities have been left to the side (Shackle 1988, 60). The capacity to set events in motion has much to do with entrepreneurship, as in Minsky's liquidity-based theory of investment, discussed earlier. I come back to this idea at the end of the present chapter, as well as in the next.

An example from the mortgage boom illustrates the role played by initiative: "CDO production was effectively on autopilot. Mortgage traders speak lovingly of 'the CDO bid.' It is mother's milk to the … market," James Grant, a market commentator, wrote in 2006. "Without it, fewer asset-backed structures could be built, and those that were would have to meet a much more conservative standard of design" (FCIC 2011, 133). So long as the presence of buyers in the market for securitizations was assured, the underlying loans could be produced quickly and without much regard for creditworthiness. The initiative of those buyers set in motion the rest of the financial machinery needed to meet their demand.

Inventories, we have seen, are what allow a dealer to respond to its customers' desires to transact. But the importance of inventories to the dealer is not they be on hand, but that they be readily accessible. A dealer can transact with its customer if it can quickly acquire what is needed to complete its side of the transaction. It is much the logic of position-making, for a dealer selling a security must be able to promptly deliver that security, just as anyone meeting a payment commitment must be able to do it promptly. To respond to the demands of the initiative of another, that is, requires that a dealer be able to act on their own initiative: when its customer arrives, the market-maker must be able, at that moment, to obtain the funds to complete the transaction. When a liquidity taker arrives, in other words, wishing to transact, the dealer must itself become a customer to another source of liquidity, must itself become a liquidity taker.

* * *

Minsky concluded from the events of 1974–5 that not only was the US acting as a financial intermediary, a bank of the world, it was doing so unsustainably – it was an "ailing bank." If US banks could not meet the survival constraint that they faced in the offshore dollar markets, then they were failing at the business of banking. By this logic, the resolution of the Franklin National crisis should have become an opportunity to rein in the offshore business of the surviving banks. These international operations were subject to the same vulnerabilities as any banking activity, and so much the same support was needed. As the Panic of 1907 had demonstrated the need for a lender of last resort in support of the domestic banking system, and thus led to the creation of the Federal Reserve, so the Fed's interventions in support of Franklin National showed that it was no less responsible for the international dollar banking system. But then, as the obligation to intervene domestically comes with the authority to regulate domestically, so the obligation to intervene internationally should come with some obligation to restrain internationally.

> The Federal Reserve was remiss in not taking effective action after 1975 to prevent the explosive growth of the offshore deposits of American banks. However, this is water over the dam. Recriminations and apportionment of blame serve no useful present purpose. It is necessary for policy to take the huge amount of offshore dollar deposits as an initial position and develop ways to minimize their adverse effects. A banker's problem exists for the banks with offshore deposits. ... [T]hese banks individually have to be able to generate a dollar flow in their favor by either selling securities, borrowing, or decreasing their lending. If there is a generalized desire to shift from holding dollar deposits to holding

deposits denominated in another currency, then the banks individually
will be unable to generate a dollar flow in their favor. In these circumstances, either market processes or Federal Reserve actions must be
able to generate a flow of dollars to the set of all international banks
which have dollar deposits. (1978c)

The failure and bailout of Franklin National should have been
a warning, an opportunity to restrain the banking activities that
had precipitated the intervention, activities undertaken not only
by Franklin National but by US banks collectively. The US as an
accounting unit was conducting unsustainable business offshore; the
actors operating that business were the US banks, who had shown
themselves, on at least that significant occasion, to be unable to
generate the cash flows needed to meet their payment constraints.
The central bank, having had to act as lender of last resort, once
the urgency of the crisis had subsided, should have then acted as
regulator, so as to restrain the problematic business. It did not do so;
and so it would have to be prepared to act as lender of last resort for
offshore dollar banking.

\* \* \*

## Supply and demand

The theory of market-making developed in the preceding sections
fits naturally with the payments theory of financial capitalism
around which Minsky's work is organized: it connects the
behavior of dealers to the need for position-making, and shows
the relationship between liquidity and the survival constraint.
The dealer model is an alternative to the standard microeconomic
theories that begin from the equality of supply and demand,
still the basis for today's economic theory. Minsky observed that
this Walrasian approach amounts to supposing that the economy
operates on a barter basis. "[F]or all the complexity and sophisti-
cation of the world, the reigning economic theory at the time of the
Great Depression maintained that the significant behavior of the
economy could be explained and understood by assuming that the
propositions derived for a primitive barter economy are relevant"
(1974d, 31; also 1977a).

According to the Walrasian conception of markets, supply meets
demand directly; there is no place for market-makers, or for the

inventories that they use to absorb the fluctuations in buy and sell orders. Because there are no dealers, neither is there any way to talk about liquidity: it is assumed, implicitly, that liquidity is available, that if one wants to sell, a buyer will be forthcoming and vice versa; likewise, that if one wants to borrow, a lender will be forthcoming and vice versa. It is assumed that this is always the case, and so the fact that sometimes it is not the case is invisible in the terms of that theory (1977f; 1983b; Hicks 1989).

To suppose that markets are Walrasian is, Minsky observed, to assume that they are essentially barter markets, where goods are exchanged for other goods. This founding myth of economics can be traced to Adam Smith's *Wealth of Nations*, and has been faithfully adopted and updated by generations of economists since. In this myth, money emerges as an expedient to ease the inconveniences of barter. Commitment to the validity of this story, implicit and explicit, persists despite the fact that it has no basis in history – there is no evidence that widespread exchange has ever been organized in such a manner (Humphrey 1985; Graeber 2011).

Because the supply–demand approach abstracts from intermediation, it has little to say about the position-making difficulties that characterize periods of market disruption. When markets are functioning smoothly, when liquidity is abundant, they approximate this Walrasian world. Any solvent unit can raise cash by selling assets to make position. But when markets are not liquid, assets may not sell quickly, and therefore position-making may be more difficult (1964a). There is no way to express this possibility in a Walrasian market. The lacuna has practical implications: in 2008, the SEC was surprised to learn that liquidity could vanish even from what were normally the most liquid of markets – repo borrowing against Treasury collateral:

> Before the run on Bear in the repo market, the SEC's liquidity stress scenarios – also known as stress tests – had not taken account of the possibility that a firm would lose access to secured funding. According to the SEC's [divisional director Erik] Sirri, the SEC never thought that a situation would arise where an investment bank couldn't enter into a repo transaction backed by high-quality collateral including Treasuries. He told the FCIC that as the financial crisis worsened, the SEC began to see liquidity and funding risks as the most critical for the investment banks, and the SEC encouraged a reduction in reliance on unsecured commercial paper and an extension of the maturities of repo loans. (FCIC 2011, 297)

In the Walrasian paradigm, there is only supply and demand, and any imbalance between the two must be resolved with a change in the price. If there is excess supply, the issue is a lack of demand, and the price must fall to accommodate the change. During the housing boom of the early 2000s, CDO demand for mortgages ensured, in turn, the existence of buyers for homes. Home builders could count on being able to sell new homes when they wanted to, into a seemingly bottomless market. This came suddenly to an end:

> Warren Peterson, a home builder in Bakersfield, felt that he could pinpoint when the world changed to the day. Peterson built homes in an upscale neighborhood, and each Monday morning, he would arrive at the office to find a bevy of real estate agents, sales contracts in hand, vying to be the ones chosen to purchase the new homes he was building. The stream of traffic was constant. On one Saturday in November 2005, he was at the sales office and noticed that not a single purchaser had entered the building.
> He called a friend, also in the home-building business, who said he had noticed the same thing, and asked him what he thought about it.
> "It's over," his friend told Peterson. (FCIC 2011, 24)

The supply–demand view would simply say that the price will fall, or must fall, to equate supply and demand. But this misreads the situation – buyers have disappeared entirely. It is not that demand has fallen, it is that liquidity has vanished. Previously, builders could sell on their own initiative to a market replete with offers to buy. As sentiment changed, there were no buyers at any price. Shackle recognizes it as reluctance, which manifests as an unwillingness to initiate. "To be compelled to decide at once what to buy might very often be a positive embarrassment" (Shackle 1972, 202).

The implications for Minsky's theory are deep. The need to make payment, brought on by the force of the survival constraint, requires households, businesses, and governments to be able to obtain money to settle their debts. The question of survival is whether they can make position when they need to – whether they can act on their own initiative. Actors must have recourse to markets to obtain cash, and so the question is, in turn, whether markets are liquid. The supply–demand framework is inadequate to the task, because it allows no role for liquidity. Minsky's view of finance requires an understanding of intermediation that goes beyond supply and demand (1977f).

## Market liquidity, funding liquidity, and monetary liquidity

This chapter's discussion of markets has focused on dealing, while saying little of banking. A dealer, who provides liquidity to sellers by standing ready to buy, must have a ready way of obtaining money: an offer to purchase is not credible unless the prospective buyer is possessed of, or can shortly become possessed of, the needed funds. The usual way to do this is to keep some cash on hand, and to borrow more when necessary. To provide liquidity as a seller requires having a ready way of obtaining inventory. The usual way to do this is to keep some inventory on hand, to replenish inventory from transactions with customers when possible, or to buy inventory with money if necessary.

When a dealer faces offers to buy and offers to sell that largely offset one another, it may have little trouble finding either cash or inventory with which to transact. A small cash balance and a small inventory might often be enough to support market-making in tranquil times. The challenge arises when a dealer faces a run of orders on one side of the market: after buying from its customers, a dealer may run out of cash. Asked to complete another purchase, the dealer eventually finds itself with a need to make position (Treynor 1987).

For dealers to make markets, in other words, requires that they have money readily available. Dealers cannot deal if they cannot obtain short-term finance. The requirement may not be sufficient: supply disruptions, for example, might mean that a particular commodity is not forthcoming at any price. But it is almost certainly necessary: if money is scarce, it will be hard to sell anything. When it needs cash, the dealer turns, in general, to its bank. A bank stands ready, in normal times, to lend to its customers when they wish to borrow, and to borrow from them (i.e., to take their deposits) when they wish to lend (deposit). Brunnermeier and Pedersen (2009) make clear the relationship between dealers standing ready to buy and sell – *market* liquidity – and banks standing ready to borrow and lend – *funding* liquidity: the availability of funding liquidity is a precondition for the existence of market liquidity.

Noting that both securities and loans are claims by one actor on another, the inherent parallel between market and funding liquidity is plain. A bank that offers to lend on its customers' initiative is in substantially the same position as a dealer that stands ready to buy a debt security on its customers' initiative. "Banks and other financial intermediaries are merchants of debt ... [they] stand ready to furnish cash to two sets of clients: their borrowers and their depositors" (1982d, 26, 30). Banks follow Treynor's (1987) prescription exactly. They offer a price, an interest rate, at which they will lend and a lower interest rate at which they will accept deposits, and they adjust these prices to encourage transactions in their counterparties:

> In the face of a decline in demand for their output, banks will try to remain fully invested. To do this they "sweeten" accommodation terms and purchase inherited eligible paper from the open market. Both the sweetening of accommodation terms and the purchase of open market paper are subsumed into a fall in the interest rate. That is, in the time horizon being considered, bankers are quantity-maintainers and price adjusters whereas both labor markets and commodity sellers adjust quantity and maintain prices. (1967b, 276f.)

If the financial substance of banking and dealing is much the same, this is not to say that the distinction does not matter in other ways. But the distinction that matters is the institutional form taken by these two activities under today's arrangements, and not a difference in the economics of those activities. Indeed, precisely because of the institutional distinction between, on the one hand, banking as extending and repaying loans, and, on the other, banking as buying and selling debt, the liquidity crisis of 2008 took the form of a breakdown of the securities dealing system (Mehrling 2010; Grad, Mehrling, and Neilson 2011).

From the late 1990s, Lehman was heavily invested in market-based finance, building a mortgage origination arm and a securities issuance business. Initially it focused on creating these products and selling them to its clients. In 2006, however, to sustain the growth of these lines of business, the company began to make and hold longer-term investments. By the summer of that year, it found that it had to make ever greater use of its own balance sheet.

> Lehman's Aurora unit continued to originate Alt-A loans [i.e., alter-native, non-prime loans to borrowers with strong credit] after the housing market had begun to show signs of weakening. Lehman also continued to securitize mortgage assets for sale but was now holding more of them as investments. Across both the commercial and residential real estate sectors, the mortgage-related assets on

Lehman's books increased from $67 billion in 2006 to $111 billion in 2007. (FCIC 2011, 176)

Just as the California builders mentioned earlier could not sell their inventory of homes, Lehman could not sell its inventory of loans.

As banks process payments for their clients, they make markets in the liabilities of the banking system, exchanging them freely among other banks. As such they are dealers in money. Banks can finance imbalances in their buy and sell orders, they can make position, by issuing their own liabilities. Money creation, that is, is the short-term answer to the payments imbalance problem: in financial capitalism, money arises as banks make markets in the means of payment (1967a).

But banks too are faced with a survival constraint: money issuance only works if there is someone who will buy it. "Any economic unit can 'emit' money, the serious problem is to get it accepted" (1972b, 142); this is so even when the economic unit is a bank. Banks might ordinarily take it for granted that their liabilities will always be accepted, but at the height of a financial crisis it need not be so. In September 2008, "many banks refused to lend to one another; the cost of interbank lending rose to unprecedented levels" (FCIC 2011, 355). When banks cannot make position, no one can make position, and the market economy is in crisis. As dealers look to their banks for refinance, so the banks must look somewhere for refinance, to a dealer of last resort (Mehrling 2010; Grad, Mehrling, and Neilson 2011), a residual market-maker. "The residual market maker is usually (but not necessarily) the central bank" (1982d, 31).

To market liquidity, created by dealers, and funding liquidity, provided by banks, we might then add *monetary* liquidity, provided by the central bank. A dealer buys or sells by adjusting its recourse to funding liquidity from its bank; the bank borrows or lends by adjusting its recourse to the provision of monetary liquidity of the central bank. For the dealer, buying an asset entails (typically) increased borrowing (a liability to the dealer), and so an expansion of the dealer's balance sheet on both sides. For the bank, increased lending (an asset) entails increased borrowing (deposits – a liability to the bank), so again an expansion of the bank's balance sheet on both sides. For the central bank, increased lending to banks (an asset to the central bank) entails increased issuance of reserves, the residual position-making instrument (and a liability to the central bank), so once again an expansion of the central bank's balance sheet on both sides.

Just as dealers support the position-making of their customers, relying on banks to make position themselves, so banks support the position-making of dealers, relying on the central bank to make position themselves. The central bank, uniquely, can make its own position, which forms the subject of the next chapter.

* * *

The events of 1974–5 were the third financial disturbance of Minsky's professional life, and they brought to light a pattern that informed his views on the Fed's failure to act in the aftermath. The survival constraint asks whether a single institution can meet its commitments as they come due; the same question manifests also at the systemic level. Minsky gave to this process the name *validation*: will an entire structure of debt commitments be made as they come due? The issue is not the legal survival of a particular firm, or the ability of a single household to avoid bankruptcy, but rather the ensemble of financial patterns and usages, entire industries and markets, which is in question. The Federal Reserve's interventions had validated the debt structures that had brought about each crisis. This paved the way for the next cycle:

> Each time the Federal Reserve acts as a lender of last resort, it prevents some financial institution or some financial market from collapsing. When it does this, it introduces additional Federal Reserve liabilities into the economy and extends a Federal Reserve guarantee over some set of financial practices. By legitimizing financial market practices through its implicit endorsement, the Federal Reserve in 1966, 1969–70, and 1974–75 set the stage for the financing of a subsequent inflationary burst. (1980c, 32)

Lender-of-last-resort operations, Minsky saw, provided a legitimation function for sets of financial practices. The central bank's intervention in one crisis was evidence that it would act similarly in the future. Its implicit endorsement, by loosening the survival constraint around specific financial patterns as they came under stress, would confirm and support the use of those practices after the stress had subsided. This meant that each intervention exerted a powerful steering function on the development of financial relations, and so should be carefully deployed.

In the Franklin National crisis, the Fed had validated the bank's offshore business, providing its implicit endorsement to all similar business. It was a missed opportunity, in Minsky's view, to do what had been done in the Crunch of 1966. Writing in response to that earlier intervention, Minsky had found that it had succeeded by reintroducing uncertainty. "The fundamental economic law behind the Crunch is this: The only way to break an inflationary investment boom set off by an evaporation of uncertainty is to reintroduce uncertainty. This is what the Crunch did" (1968c, 44). The Federal Reserve had, Minsky thought, cut that boom down to size by showing that economic prosperity was not a foregone conclusion. It had tightened credit at an opportune moment, prompting lenders into recognition of uncertainty, thus quelling speculative activity. The problem with the Franklin intervention, eight years later, was that the Fed had failed to extract any price for its intervention.

The Fed had validated US banks' offshore business, and so had taken some responsibility for backstopping it; having acted in support of Franklin National, it would be hard to leave banks to the consequences of their lending decisions when next they faced trouble. As Franklin receded into memory, the problem presented itself in another form, as Minsky observed the mounting inflation of the late 1970s. Tightening the availability of credit to restrain inflation would put firms' survival in jeopardy. The entire debt structure had been built around rising prices. The Fed could validate that structure, supporting and sustaining the financing activity and thus the resulting inflation; or it could constrain it, risking bankruptcies and recession. "The Federal Reserve therefore is in a dilemma. ... [I]t can bring a halt to an inflationary process only as it forces high enough interest rates so that units which need refinancing are found to be ineligible for financing in the market because of inadequate expected profits or cash flows" (1980c, 35).

The nub of the Fed's dilemma was that it found itself constrained, forced to act, and therefore powerless to rein in overextended debt. The survival constraint limits borrowers only if it is sometimes expected to bind; anxiety about sometimes not being able to make position must be sufficient to guide them into prudent action beforehand. If the Fed has given its implicit assurance that it will validate a debt structure, then, at least at the aggregate level, the possibility of financial failure loses its power to guide activity. The events from the mid-1970s to the mid-1980s led Minsky to see that an essential feature of the central bank's task was to maintain its initiative. An efficient banking system was "a system in which the ability of banks to force the Federal Reserve's hand by means of periodic threats of failure is attenuated" (1985c, 18).

\* \* \*

## Interpreting Keynes

Minsky saw his work as building on that of John Maynard Keynes, an effort that received its fullest statement in his (1975c) book *John Maynard Keynes*. Minsky argued that Keynes's most significant insights had been lost by the main lines of interpretation within the economics profession, and presented his own view as "unreconstructed" Keynesianism. This view takes shape over the course of articles preceding and following the 1975 book (1972a; 1972b; 1972c; 1973b; 1974b; 1985f), as well as the (1986e) *Stabilizing an Unstable Economy*. Minsky felt he was recovering a dimension of Keynes's thought that had been lost; I argued earlier that he found in Keynes a sympathetic medium in which to express ideas that were very much his own.

In this section I will offer some small contribution to an understanding of this by sketching an argument that leads from the central themes of the theory of financial capitalism developed here – uncertainty, initiative, and liquidity – to the work of Keynes via a small number of secondary sources, which constitute my recommendation of where to start on Keynes (Shackle 1972; Shackle 1988; Hicks 1989). (Minsky was aware of Shackle's work but would have benefited, I think, from more engagement (1977f); the mature Hicks, which I cite here, has come a long way from the younger Hicks of IS–LM.)

Keynes's is a theory of an uncertain world. "The one big thing in Keynes's ultimate conception is our unknowledge of what will create itself in time-to-come. 'We simply do not know'" (Shackle 1988, 196; also Keynes 1936; Keynes 1937). This is a principal point of divergence between Keynes and his interpreters among the economists, for such unknowledge is quite the opposite of the determinacy and calculability of equilibrium that have been the endpoint of many of those interpretations. It is that much more remarkable – as Shackle notes – that Keynes, himself the author of *A Treatise on Probability*, concluded that statistics could not resolve this ignorance.

Keynes maintains that the world is inescapably uncertain, and that economic fluctuations follow from actors' responses to that uncertainty. "To buy the means (natural resources, produced facilities and human work) of producing goods is to gamble on the eventual sale value of those goods. From time to time businessmen can lose their nerve and refuse this gamble, preferring to keep their wealth in money rather than embark it in the products of employment" (Shackle 1988, 78). Those receiving payment inflows, that is, might choose to accumulate money rather than generating cash outflows. When this choice is made on a sufficient scale, it is enough to explain the cyclical movements of the economy.

Keynes's theory is centered, that is, on the initiative of entrepreneurs, their willingness to set economic activity in motion by allocating cash flows to investment. Initiative, in the argument of the present book, is effective when it is met with liquidity – when the desire to transact is met with the opportunity to transact. Minsky interpreted this through the pricing of capital assets – the desire to hold money now decreases the demand price for capital assets, which promise flows of payment only in the future; it also increases the supply price of investment goods, as the financing of their production requires cash now (1975c; 1980e; Mehrling 1999). This "two-price" theory was Minsky's interpretation of Keynes's theory of liquidity preference.

Keynes, however, was inconsistent in his own treatment of liquidity. So far, I have followed Minsky in taking the word to refer, when describing an economic actor, to the ability to force a unit of cash flow in one's favor and, when describing a market, to the condition in which exchange for money is readily conducted. Keynes's earlier *A Treatise on Money* (Keynes 1930, II: 67) thinks of liquidity similarly: "more certainly realizable at short notice without loss." Of this definition, Hicks makes clear that "realizable" means convertible into money, for the purposes of meeting cash commitments; "loss" is the loss due to sale at an inopportune moment, thus the concessionary sale that would be made only under the press of the survival constraint (Hicks 1989).

A security offers liquidity when it is readily exchanged for cash, a transient state of affairs that depends on market conditions. By the time of *The General Theory*, however, Keynes's usage had drifted; the transience of liquidity of any particular market gives way to what seems to be an inherent characteristic of some securities and not others. It follows that what is missing from *The General Theory* is a theory of liquidity provision – a theory of market-making (Hicks 1989). Minsky recognizes the incompatibility: "[T]he doctrines of Walras, which are based upon market clearing, and of Keynes, which are based upon investing behavior, are incompatible; the neo-classical synthesis is internally inconsistent" (1981c, 200).

Neither the mathematical theories offered by Keynes himself, nor those mathematical interpretations offered by later economists, really address this inconsistency. Minsky took many theoretical stabs at the problem. Mostly in his early work, he tried to capture systemic instability using institutional ceilings and floors in accelerator–multiplier models (1954; 1957b; 1959a; 1959b; 1962; 1965b; 1965d; Minsky and Ferri 1984). But he concluded that the effort was hopeless: "such a mechanical explanation of the business cycle is inconsistent with the major thrust of Keynes's views" (1975c, 30). The IS–LM framework gets much shorter shrift: a world with stable supply and demand for money, he said, is a world without crisis, and so it is not much like our world (1972a). No major economic modeling effort has managed a serious treatment of liquidity: "*Liquidity* is a denial of the rationality of the only economic world we have evolved" (Shackle 1972, 165, emphasis original).

Minsky was not alone in feeling that something essential had been lost in economists' absorption of Keynes's insights. In the years following the publication of *John Maynard Keynes*, Minsky allied himself with other dissidents, and in particular with the post-Keynesians. Their shared outsider status was certainly a factor, but there was also evidently some effort at intellectual engagement. In a number of texts over this period, Minsky explored his status as a post-Keynesian. He recognized an affinity, particularly in the rejection of what had become mainstream Keynesianism. "The financial instability hypothesis is a variant of post-Keynesian economics. The interpretation of Keynes that has descended from the formalisations by Hicks, Hansen, Modigliani and Patinkin of *The General Theory* has always been of questionable legitimacy" (1978d, 3).

Despite this shared critique, Minsky had not shied away from dismissing post-Keynesian efforts to grapple with uncertainty. His (1974b) review of *Money and the Real World* notes that Paul Davidson makes room for uncertainty, but the review comes across as dismissive. The jabs are directed at foes as much as allies – Minsky seems to have settled on the financial instability hypothesis, connected it to Keynes, and used that stance to object to all other approaches (1974f). "[E]conomists have much to be humble about" (1974d, 30). His engagements with the post-Keynesians are consistently ambivalent. He described the label as "unfortunate" (1978d, 3) and said that it had "lost its power to identify" (1981c, 199). He seems, nonetheless, to have felt that they were a potentially receptive audience that could be brought along. He was reluctantly willing to describe his own work as post-Keynesian, as long as that could mean what he wanted it to mean: "My 'brand' of Post-Keynesian analysis emphasizes cash flows" (1988a, 26; also 1977d; 1977f; 1981e; Ferri and Minsky 1989; Minsky and Campbell 1990).

The approach that follows such characterizations is no different from what Minsky had been doing all along. "The post-Keynesians hold that the serious study of money requires a turning away from the Arrow–Debreu structure and the building of a theory that starts from the role of money in financing accumulation and the effect upon the system functioning of asset values and liability structures" (1985a, 5). He goes on to describe his own financial instability hypothesis. Despite his clearly expressed ambivalence, Minsky's attachment to Keynes, his emphasis on the determinants of investment, and the central place he gives to time and uncertainty mean that he could reasonably be grouped among the post-Keynesians (Lavoie 2006). But his message does not seem really to have been heard – there is no place in post-Keynesian theory for the survival constraint, for position-making, or for a notion of transient liquidity.

The post-Keynesians themselves have not been hesitant to claim Minsky as one of their own. The synthesis of Lavoie (2006) includes a narrative of Minsky's financial instability hypothesis, which I mention again later. Lavoie captures the idea that stability is destabilizing, the "paradox of tranquillity" as he calls it, which is certainly consonant with the idea as Minsky put it. But Minsky was at pains to express his ideas in terms of cash flows, which are absent in Lavoie's version as they are largely absent in post-Keynesian macroeconomics in general. Without cash flows, the post-Keynesian notion of liquidity cannot be connected to the liquidity-generating activities of intermediaries. Minsky is adopted, it seems, for his sympathetic conclusions, but without the reasoning by which he came to them. His brand of post-Keynesianism, he stated, was about cash flows; it must be said that he did not really succeed in bending post-Keynesians to that view. Still, Minsky was present as early as his 1969–70 sabbatical and at gatherings in the early 1970s of what would come to be called post-Keynesian economists. He contributed (1978b) to the very first issue of the *Journal of Post-Keynesian Economics*. His participation in the project was sustained and so surely sympathetic and productive, even if he did not win converts to his financial view of capitalism.

At a few years' distance, Minsky's engagement with Keynes seems largely unfulfilled. Minsky's key insights are independent; they are visible already in his early work, before they are framed as unreconstructed Keynesianism (e.g. 1957a; 1964b). Nonetheless, he was quite correct about the basic identity between his argument and that of Keynes: for both, uncertainty means that initiative may be insufficient. Minsky correctly sought to connect this to the pattern of cash commitments that arise as an expression of that uncertainty – to the financial structure. These commitments drive position-making and thus the need for liquidity, but Keynes's treatment of liquidity was insufficiently rich to match Minsky's sense of the financial mechanics.

# 6

# *Last resort*

## The endpoint of position-making

The first serious disruption in financial markets since the Great Depression, and the first of Minsky's career as an economist, the Credit Crunch of 1966, was brought to an end through the intervention of the Federal Reserve in August of that year. Struggling to make position, banks had started selling off their holdings of debt securities issued by state and local governments. Limited liquidity in these markets meant that prices fell quite sharply, but the banks were desperate for cash and were short of alternative instruments by which to raise it. The Fed ended the panic with a letter on August 23 of that year.

The letter changed the central bank's stance toward the markets. Where it had been maintaining relatively tight money, it switched decisively at that moment to a stance of accommodation, seeking the restoration of "orderly money market conditions and the moderation of unusual liquidity pressures." Not only that; the Fed asked banks to stop liquidating municipal securities, and instead to raise cash by allowing loans to businesses to run off. It agreed to provide financial support to banks that did so. "It is recognized that banks adjusting their positions through loan curtailment may at times need a longer period of discount accommodation than would be required for the disposition of securities" (Board of Governors of the Federal Reserve System 1967, 103; Wolfson 1986).

In 1966, the Fed finally stepped in when the market for municipal (muni) securities became disorganized. Banks were making position by selling anxiously into the market, even as those sales came at steepening discounts. The Fed put a stop to it by providing cash on better terms, and assuring banks that they would be able to refinance until the difficulties had subsided. Thus the meaning of "last resort": the Fed would not tolerate the disruption of the muni market, and so it created another option. By pricing it more cheaply, the Fed ensured that it would be taken up. The banks, confident of their own access to cash, were again willing to lend to others (1986e).

Many times over the following decades, Minsky would observe the capacity of the Federal Reserve to end a panic by intervention in financial markets. The obligation of the central bank to act as lender of last resort was already well established. Walter Bagehot's (1873) prescription for how to end a liquidity crisis was well known; Henry Thornton (1802; Hicks 1989) had said it even earlier. It was the dramatic intervention of J. P. Morgan – a private citizen – as lender of last resort in the Panic of 1907 that had motivated the creation of a central bank for the United States, the Federal Reserve, to serve as a public institution capable of doing that job (Hughes 1986).

The Fed is also responsible for some aspects of bank regulation, and for non-crisis interventions in financial markets, but Minsky placed the central bank's function as lender of last resort above all else. This view is closely connected to the payments theory of financial capitalism that has been developed in the preceding chapters. The present chapter locates the central bank in that theory as a way of understanding its distinctive capacity to intervene at the height of crisis. This, in turn, helps extend the theory up to its full institutional form.

* * *

Minsky's last major project, the 1986 *Stabilizing an Unstable Economy*, is largely continuous with his work of the previous decades. It is an expansive effort, the two most substantive parts being an empirical study of the Franklin National crisis and a restatement of the theoretical components of *John Maynard Keynes*. Two smaller parts provide what read as a series of topical essays on banking, inflation, and various policy proposals. Read on its own, the volume is at times disorienting in its breadth, its repetitiveness, and the tendency for key insights to be buried among unrelated discursions.

It seems better advised to read the book as a step in Minsky's intellectual journey, a further refinement of the ideas that had occupied him for three decades, a final rehearsal of the major insights and perspectives he had been developing since his dissertation. In this regard, the breadth of the book has the feel of an archive or an autobiography, an attempt to capture every contribution in a single place: a short section on "An employment strategy" rehashes Minsky's conclusions from his work on the War on Poverty; a couple of pages on industrial policy recall the entrepreneurial capitalism of Henry Simons. The reason the arguments feel repetitive, perhaps, is that each foray reflects an underlying perspective more than it reflects the details of the case at hand. With a bit of distance, it is perhaps easier to see that it is for this underlying perspective – that is, his theory of financial capitalism – that Minsky should be remembered.

Minsky's frustrations with the economics discipline had matured and stabilized without diminishing. His own view had crystallized: the critiques of marginalism and the absence of finance are as present in 1986 as in his 1954 dissertation; they appear alongside the failings of monetarism and mainstream Keynesianism, expressed most systematically in the 1975 book. Minsky marks time with crises – 1966, 1970, 1974–5, and now also 1980 and 1982; but now that timeline notes not only the financial history but also his own place in it. Interest and attention to his work, Minsky's moments of opportunity to sway the discipline, rise at those turning points, and fall away after:

> As a previous crisis recedes in time, it is quite natural for central bankers, government officials, bankers, businessmen, and even economists to believe that a new era has arrived. Cassandra-like warnings that nothing basic has changed, that there is a financial breaking point that will lead to a deep depression, are naturally ignored in these circumstances. Since the doubters do not have fashionable printouts to prove the validity of their views, it is quite proper for established authority to ignore arguments drawn from unconventional theory, history, and institutional analysis. Nevertheless ... the successful functioning of an economy within an initially robust financial structure will lead to a structure that becomes more fragile as time elapses. ([1986e] 2008, 237f.)

The "Cassandra-like warnings" he refers to are evidently Minsky's own: he is offering, as autobiography, a meta-theory of the economics discipline. Post-crisis forgetting is enough to relegate the warnings of future crisis to the margins. That these warnings are consistent over time is not an argument in their favor but rather an excuse for the discipline to disregard them; the leanings of the business, policy, and academic elite are served by the belief that things have changed for the better. The doubters refuse on principle to conform to the methodological strictures – the "printouts" of econometric analysis – because these are based on a theory that makes instability impossible; yet for that same refusal their warnings are disregarded. But the clock keeps ticking – crisis always recurs, irregularly perhaps, and Minsky stands by his theory.

* * *

The urgency of crisis, as we have seen, comes from the survival constraint – maturing commitments to be paid. The central bank's intervention is the endpoint of a series: "last resort" follows "next-to-last resort," and so on. In 1966, banks first sought cash by selling into the more liquid market for Treasuries, and only then into the less liquid market for municipal securities (Wolfson 1986). As the need deepens, borrowers are forced to pay for access to ever-more-valuable hoards of cash – the largest, the most reliable. As the height of the crisis approaches, owners of such hoards value them increasingly highly, and part with them only at a high price. Those in need must pay these high prices, as long as are able, lest they put their survival in jeopardy. The options are exhausted as needed, each more expensive than the last.

The logic is that of position-making, but this is not the everyday matching of cash inflows and outflows. When the need is a cash shortfall specific not to an actor or even a group of actors, but to the entire system, to many actors or most actors or all actors, then the system itself is in crisis. "Precise definitions are not necessary, for the major episodes of instability, whether runaway inflation, a speculative bubble, an exchange crisis, or debt deflation, can be identified by pointing" (1982d, 13). In 2008,

> "[y]ou had a broad-based run on commercial paper markets," [former New York Fed president and then-Treasury Secretary Timothy] Geithner told the FCIC. "And so you faced the prospect of some of the largest companies in the world and the United States losing the capacity to fund and access those commercial paper markets." Three decades of easy borrowing for those with top-rated credit in a very liquid market had disappeared almost overnight. The panic threatened to disrupt the payments system through which financial institutions transfer trillions of dollars in cash and assets every day and upon which consumers rely – for example, to use their credit cards and debit cards. "At that point, you don't need to map out which particular mechanism – it's not relevant anymore – it's

become systemic and endemic and it needs to be stopped," [the Fed's Michael] Palumbo said. (FCIC 2011, 358f.)

When the payment system ceases to function, the problem is not that an actor, or even many actors, cannot make position. The problem, at that point, is that position-making itself is called into question. Without venturing a definition, a characteristic of crisis is that the need reaches to the most central mechanism of financial capitalism, the payment system. Without payment, no survival constraint can be met.

Yet, as Minsky saw and as we shall see, the central bank can bring an end to this process. Even when the survival constraint binds for the system as a whole, even when the largest banks are threatened, the central bank retains the ability to act.

\* \* \*

One of the main purposes of *Stabilizing an Unstable Economy* is to interpret the events surrounding the Franklin National crisis; despite the Cassandra-like warnings, the episode had led to a major economic downturn, and, for Minsky, to a new round of questions. An important one surrounded the vulnerability of the system to position-making difficulties. Minsky saw an increase in the complexity of the financial system: not just more types of security and markets, but greater variation in how position-making was carried out.

> We now have a banking system in which normal functioning depends upon a wide variety of money-market instruments being available for position-making. Since the end of World War II, the banking system has evolved from the simplicity of the Treasury bill's monopoly as *the* position-making instrument to a complex situation in which a representative bank juggles its government-security account or its federal funds position, has large denomination certificates of deposit, repurchase agreements, Eurodollar borrowings (or sales), and borrowings at the Federal Reserve. The behavior of a system with such a variety of position-making possibilities is quite different from that of a simple system in which the Treasury-security market monopolized position-making activity. Furthermore, techniques for position-making are still evolving. ([1986e] 2008, 86, emphasis original)

That banks would resort to a range of different markets in their search for cash need not, in and of itself, create undue difficulties. Where one market functions, two might as well. Minsky worried, however, about how that position-making would come to an end, in crisis. There could be a variety of position-making instruments only because, in normal times, they were more or less substitutes: a marginal loan in federal funds, repo, or Eurodollars would come at essentially the same interest rate. But they are different instruments that trade on different markets, and the close connection between their prices is maintained by arbitrage relationships. These in turn depend on actors' being able to simultaneously transact in each market, to carry out that arbitrage, and thus keep the prices in line.

Minsky's concern, then, has very much to do with the existence and stability of the dealer system, which connects the various money markets one to the other. In the event of unusual position-making difficulties, the money markets as a whole would come under strain, heightened demand for liquidity would challenge dealer balance sheets, and the ability of the central bank to serve as lender of last resort would be made more difficult by the complexity of these interlinkages.

* * *

## Centrality and discretion

In a financial capitalist system, one must pay one's debts. Debts are paid when one delivers money, but what constitutes money depends on the circumstances. In practice, most debts are settled, most payments are made, by the exchange of claims on a third party. One might complete a retail transaction by relinquishing claims on a bank and transferring them to the credit of the retailer. To hand over banknotes is to transfer ownership of claims on the issuing bank. Payment is relative, not final: the seller feels that they have been paid because of their confidence of being able, in turn, to use the claim they have received as payment for something else (Hicks 1989).

This relativity means that payment is necessarily hierarchical. Payment requires the transfer of claims on actors who are higher in the system, or, we might say, more central. Though the transfer of claims on a retail bank may be suitably final for a transaction between individuals or small firms, it will not do for transactions between banks. Such a transaction requires the transfer of a higher claim. This ranking gives structure to the payment system; at the very center is the central bank, claims on which are the means of payment for debts between the largest commercial banks (1957a).

What is money at the center is money everywhere; the reverse is not true. The central bank is the issuer of the ultimate means of payment, the money that clears payments *regardless* of who are the transactors, *regardless* of where one is in the system. The actor who can issue the means of final settlement is unique in the financial capitalist system: it can loosen the survival constraint, for anyone else, at its discretion. If a counterparty of the Fed needs funds to meet a payment commitment, the Fed, and only the Fed, can create those funds. It can extend a loan outright, or purchase an asset of any kind to do so – what matters is that claims on the Fed are money everywhere, and so are sure to ease the survival constraint.

Minsky found this power to be the defining feature of centrality. "In its very essence the central bank is the operator of the discretionary element in the financial system" (1964a, 271). As the survival constraint tightens for the system as a whole, options may begin to close for many actors. In the hierarchical payment system, however, the actor at the center does not lose its ability to act. This is why the central bank can serve as lender of last resort – even when all others find that their hands are tied, the central bank has room to maneuver. After the rescue of Franklin National, the scope of the US central bank's role as lender of last resort had even extended beyond national boundaries. Offshore dollars are, in the end, promises to pay in New York. Because of the Fed's presence in the New York markets, the US central bank affects the terms on which dollars are available to the world, so it is "the *de facto* lender of last resort to the international financial structure" (1985c, 15).

This power is immense, but it is not absolute. It is constrained by the issuing capacity of the central bank, which therefore must protect this capacity. Paraphrasing British economist R. S. Sayers, Minsky said "it is the duty of every bank and most of all of a central bank, to be rich." He elaborated: "Being rich means that a bank [or] central bank ... has the power to force a 'cash flow' in its favor (i.e., to make its liabilities scarce) without imposing costs that are too high on itself and on its debtors" (1986a, 8; also 1981a).

In the terms of chapter 5, this is to say that the central bank must remain liquid. This is not a sure thing, though its central position means that illiquidity has a different appearance for the Fed than for other actors. Minsky was attuned, for example, to the danger of a high cost of issuance for a Federal Reserve that, after the Franklin National crisis, had to keep its eye on the liquidity of international dollar markets without giving up responsibility for domestic money markets in the US. Forced to intervene in a crisis to support domestic institutions, the central bank could find that its ability to force a cash flow internationally was reduced (1986a).

Writing earlier, before Franklin National, Minsky had described a similar bind on the Fed's freedom to act in different terms: "The banker role of the United States means that interest rates in New York must be high enough so that a 'covered' move abroad of short-term funds is not profitable" (1965a, 11). Crisis enters hypothetically, as the consequence of a precipitous withdrawal of short-term funds.

A different risk to the central bank's liquidity could come if its actions were anticipated, making the cost of forcing a cash flow in its favor high: "If its pattern of behavior with respect to events such as the existence of excess supply or excess demand is too well known, then other units will operate on the basis of what they expect the central bank to do" (1964a, 271). Anticipating intervention by the Fed, other actors trade ahead of it, using up liquidity and increasing the scale of the interventions required to achieve the target of the intervention.

The central bank's power allows it to act when others cannot; so, Minsky argued, it should not act when others can. He objected to the Fed's practice, in the early 1960s, of daily intervention – "high-level busywork" – in the money markets. The Fed should not transact on its own initiative while the banking system still has other options: "Assuming that the Federal Reserve System would behave 'like a central bank should' if a financial crisis did develop, the unnecessary defensive operations are seen as premature [lender-of-last-resort] operations" (1963b, 411; also 1983c). Banks can access their own position-making instruments in response to their customers' demands for cash, and the central bank should step in by creating reserves only when banks can no longer do so. To do otherwise was to risk the central bank's actions being expected and relied upon, and so giving up its initiative.

Its discretion is a distinguishing characteristic of the central bank, and in a crisis, when it is the only actor who retains initiative, this fact comes to the fore. But Minsky's is a theory of financial capitalism for normal times as well as for crisis times: the survival constraint always looms, even if it does not usually bind so tightly as in a panic. That the central bank, at the center of the payment system, retains the ability to act on its own initiative is not only a guide for in-crisis policy; it is not that the central bank switches from normal policy-making to crisis resolution and then back. For Minsky, tranquil times are better regarded as an opportunity to anticipate and avoid the next crisis: "Because the Federal Reserve has the responsibility, so to speak, to pick up the pieces when things go wrong, it must be concerned with and guide the growth and evolution of financial practices in periods of tranquility as well as when circumstance forces it to intervene" ([1986e] 2008, 45).

Financial evolution during good economic times is enabled by innovation and motivated by the desire to economize on reserves. The pattern of cash commitments that results will eventually strain the capacity of the system for position-making. When that strain becomes crisis, it will fall to the central bank to loosen the survival constraint and allow normal functioning to return; and so its attention must turn to that pattern of cash commitments as it unfolds.

\* \* \*

In the changing practices by which banks maintained their reserve balances, Minsky saw a growing gap between the central bank and the commercial banks. Federal Reserve practices had evolved, by the time he was writing *Stabilizing an Unstable Economy*, to be based on open-market transactions. To add or drain reserves from the banking system, the central bank would buy and sell securities, mostly Treasury securities. When the Fed purchased a Treasury bill from the market, it would create new reserves to complete the trade, adding to the system's total level of reserve balances; likewise, when it sold bonds to the market, it would destroy reserves in the corresponding amount.

Such open-market transactions come on the initiative of the Fed, but they depend on the existence of willing counterparties to complete the transaction. This the Fed ensured with the cultivation of a group of so-called primary dealers, who were obliged to offer a quote whenever the Fed wished to transact, and who benefited from the almost daily flow of open-market transactions that the Fed conducted. The typical transaction was a sale-and-repurchase agreement in Treasuries, which made use both of the Fed's inventory of government debt and of the thriving repo markets that supported the growing securities-based credit system. Minsky saw the shift to open-market operations as diminishing the banking relationship between commercial banks and their central bank:

> If bank reserves are largely the result of discounting short-term paper tied to the ownership of business inventories, then as loans fall due and

are repaid bank reserve balances fall. To bring reserves to target levels, banks would have to discount paper and there would be a continuing business relation between banks and the Federal Reserve. Thus, a *major* necessary reform is for the Federal Reserve to shift from the open-market technique to discounting. The discount window method for creating the reserve base induces favorable terms for the hedge financing of short-term positions and blunts the tendency toward fragile financing structures. ([1986e] 2008, 361f., emphasis original)

Under a discount-window system, banks came to the Federal Reserve with their short-term business credit and received cash for it. As with open-market operations, the result was the creation of reserves. As Minsky notes, however, the use of the discount window could more directly support stable financing arrangements: knowing what paper would be acceptable to the Fed, the banks would choose to extend credit in support of hedge financing structures, those in which drains on cash can readily be matched with sources of cash. It would be a notable reduction in the stigma associated with the use of the discount window: the predominance of open-market operations for adjusting reserve balances had gone alongside an understanding that resort to the discount window implied that a bank was at serious risk. In proposing a more routine, less stigmatized discount window, Minsky surely had in mind Schumpeter's *ephor* of capitalism:

In *The Theory of Economic Development* Schumpeter called the banker/ financier the *ephor* of market economies. The *ephor* was a magistrate of Sparta who contained and controlled the Kings. In Schumpeter's vision it is the banking structure of a capitalist economy which controls and delineates what can be financed, and only that which is financed enters the realm of the possible. ... In the present stage of development the financiers are not acting as the *ephors* of the economy, editing the financing that takes place so that the development of the economy is promoted. Today's managers of money are but little concerned with the development of the capital assets of an economy. (1993c, 106, 113)

By promoting stable finance through the discount window, Minsky thought, the Federal Reserve could act as the *ephor* of the financial system. Central-bank collateral policy, the statement of what paper would be eligible for discount, would guide the evolution of cash commitments for the system as a whole. Making the discount window the normal mode of bank refinance would create a little lender of last resort, not only for systemic crisis but for the normal situations when the survival constraint binds or may soon bind. Everyday use of the discount window would also mean that when refinancing difficulties eventually did become widespread, the facility for extending credit would already be in place – only an expansion of the volume of discount window lending would be needed.

\* \* \*

## Validation

At the center of financial capitalism is the payment system, and at the center of the payment system is the central bank. Its position at the epicenter means that the central bank is able to loosen the survival constraint, and so it is uniquely able to act at its own discretion, even when liquidity is hard to come by elsewhere in the system. To be able to ease the burden of payment is an immense power, the deployment of which demands careful consideration.

For Henry Simons, recall, such power was in contradiction to the ideals of liberalism; he wanted to make it unnecessary by freeing the entire system from the burden of the survival constraint: he sought to eliminate payment fixed in nominal quantity, or to eliminate payment due at a certain time. Freed from the burden of position-making, the financial system would have no need for a central bank. Simons, that is, wanted to eliminate the discretionary element from central banking, "to design and establish with the greatest intelligence a monetary system good enough so that, hereafter, we may hold to it unrationally – on faith – as a religion, if you please" (Simons 1948, 169).

From the point of view of the theory developed here, it is a contradiction to attempt to reduce central banking to a mechanical rule: it would be a forfeiture of the very characteristic that distinguishes it. A central bank that must pre-commit to a set of policies, come what may, has no initiative at all; it has signed away its discretion to act as it sees fit at the moment when it is needed. For Minsky, instead, the central bank's discretion could provide an institutional counterbalance to the systemic excesses of financial capitalism. He saw the central bank's power as one that must be lived with. "The best we can hope for," he said in reply to Simons, "is not a rule but an awareness of how complex is the task of an authority possessing discretion" (1967b, 294).

The task is indeed complex, and Minsky spent a great deal of time thinking about how it might be done well. The financial structure, the configuration of commitments to pay, unfolds over time as promises are made and then, eventually, either kept or broken. The central bank can, at its discretion, support the financial structure by supporting some of those promises, serving as a source of the means of payment when none other is forthcoming (Brimmer 1989). This gives it a measure of control over how that structure develops, and so it might, *contra* Simons, be possible to guide it with discretion, not by rules only, in support of some social purpose.

* * *

The crisis of 1975 was resolved without exacting a major toll on society more broadly, and this fact motivated Minsky's detailed analysis of the events of that crisis. His conclusions were not a sharp break, but rather were incremental advances on what he had argued after past financial disturbances. The presence of the central bank as a lender of last resort is a central feature of the analysis. The idea of validation captures the relationship, not between the central bank and the institutions in crisis, but between the character of the intervention and the nature of the debt structures that had precipitated it. Debt always entails the question of default, the uncertainty about the borrower's future that must leave at least some doubt about their ability to pay, and validation is a powerful answer to that question.

> In each case, the Federal Reserve, because it has the ultimate weapon for validating a debt structure – namely the ability to create Federal Reserve liabilities – had to play an overt or covert role, often substituting its liabilities for those of private banks or other private borrowers. But the Federal Reserve's power to create money need not be used in every instance; a lender-of-last-resort problem can be handled indirectly by letting it be known that Federal Reserve credit would be available if necessary. It is important to emphasize that, because the Federal Reserve System is directly or indirectly the lender of last resort to the financial system as it exists, any constraint placed on Federal Reserve flexibility (e.g., by mandating mechanical rules of behavior) attenuates its power to act. Rules cannot substitute for lender-of-last-resort discretion. ([1986e] 2008, 62)

The ability of the central bank to influence financial structures derives from its ability to act – its "ultimate weapon" – and it is this power that allows it to resolve systemic doubts about payment. Federal Reserve liabilities are the claims whose transfer, uniquely, can resolve debts anywhere in the payment system; the ability to create them at its own discretion is why the central bank can serve as lender of last resort in the first place. Such intervention – the timely creation of federal funds and their allocation to where the survival constraint binds most urgently – is sufficiently potent that even indirect assurances that central-bank refinance *would* be forthcoming may be enough to resolve a crisis. But then, for Minsky, to constrain that very ability by requiring the Fed to conform only to rules would be to cut off the very means by which the instability of capitalism can be smoothed out.

There are echoes of Schumpeter throughout the 1986 book; though his name is mentioned only in the preface and in a footnote, Minsky wrote several pieces in later years that would sort out his intellectual connection to the man who would have been his dissertation supervisor. Without citation, Minsky's observations about the role of the central bank in validating debt structures nonetheless have much to do with Schumpeter:

> [a] central bank, being the "ultimate creator of credit," is exempt from the limitations banking practice imposes on member banks, and hence, in the absence of those legal restrictions and traditions, would enjoy almost unlimited freedom in acting on business situations. Quite apart from the fact that government could never afford to allow it to fail, it need not bother about "quality" and "purpose" of credit at all, since it would have it in its power to improve any "quality" and to justify – in the business sense – any "purpose" to any desired extent by further creation of balances. ... Member banks are distinct centers of economic decision. No policy of the central bank, short of a declaration to sanction and make good the consequences of any action whatsoever, can alter all the data on which such decisions rest and, in particular, the logic of the banking business ... [T]here is a long way from action in the central market to action on the money market in our sense, and a still longer one from this to action on business activity and prices. Even legally unlimited power to create balances does not imply actual power to create them, still less the power to make them active. (Schumpeter 1939, 654)

Schumpeter imbues the central bank with much the same capacities as does Minsky: its power to validate debt by the creation of reserve balances gives it immense sway over the financial system. The perhaps exuberantly described "unlimited freedom" it has in validating debt, however, is tempered by the long distance between affecting conditions of refinance and affecting business conditions.

\* \* \*

As individual commitments to pay are tested by the survival constraint, so the entire financial structure is subject to *validation*: actors in the financial system make promises to pay – more or less rash promises according to their understanding of their future prospects. Their lenders express their own understanding of the future by their willingness to lend. The resulting debt structures, systemic configurations of promises to pay, are validated if they are indeed paid as promised when the due date arrives. When a preponderance of individual borrowers fulfill their payment obligations, the systemic arrangements under which those obligations were made are reinforced.

This *ex post* confirmation of *ex ante* optimism confirms the wisdom of all concerned, and fuels, in turn, further optimism. Early validation of new financial usages – new securities, new markets – encourages their further adoption. The ideal situation, for Minsky, was debt supporting entrepreneurial activity. When such investments are successful, they yield an excess of cash inflows over cash outflows; in aggregate, this provides the means by which the debt structure can be validated (1980a). Minsky made frequent use of an arguably idiosyncratic interpretation of Kalecki's essay "The Determinants of Profits" (Kalecki 1971, 78–92) in support of this view. Investment spending creates profit flows, says Kalecki; profit flows validate debt structures, adds Minsky; so business debt structures are stable when they go to support investment.

This view has implications for the role of the central bank. One proposal was to use the last-resort function of the central bank to selectively validate patterns of business finance. "We should once again try to move to a central bank-member bank structure in which a major part of central bank assets are of business-related paper" (1984b, 39). The central bank can ease the survival constraint for others, at its discretion. So let it provide a stable source of refinancing against business debt, so that validation is directed toward the most economically productive lending. Tying the central bank to investment flows, Minsky thought, would support an entrepreneurial capitalism not unlike that envisioned by Simons (1966b; 1985c).

One way or another, the central bank's support would validate debt structures; better to point it toward those that encouraged production, because the alternative would be to support unsustainable finance. Writing at the time of the 1984 crisis, Minsky criticized intervention on behalf of troubled bank Continental Illinois on just such lines. Continental had overextended itself in lending to business, and to make position was seeking funding in offshore dollar markets (Wolfson 1986). Minsky objected to a coordinated rescue from the Fed, the Comptroller of the Currency, and the FDIC: "A program that capitalizes interest and guarantees to monetize debts if necessary will quickly lead to another run from the dollar" (1984d). By funding debts without exercising its discretion, the Federal Reserve was validating unsustainable financing patterns and putting the centrality of the dollar itself at risk.

Validation would rather have to go alongside guidance of the unfolding of financing relationships. In a large, complex financial system, Minsky thought, major institutions should be able to count on liquidity support. "[N]o financial institutions of the significance of the life insurance companies should be allowed to exist without a guaranteed refinancing source" (1964a, 183), and not just life insurance companies. But the essential role for private financial institutions in the system's evolving financial structure would mean that guaranteed refinance would require steering of the underlying borrowing and lending; by selectively validating stable structures, the central bank could use its discretion to exert some influence over the evolution of those structures.

The central bank, that is, must look ahead to the possibility of future crisis and an obligation to intervene, and working backward to the present, it must interact with the pre-crisis financial structure to support stability. Can judicious use of the power of the central bank avoid crisis altogether?

* * *

The Fed's position at the center of the payment system is unique, but it is not the only entity that is capable of mustering financial resources in difficult times. Minsky observed, in the Franklin National crisis, that the increase in government spending had much to do with the mildness of the recession. So-called automatic stabilizers, spending programs such as Social Security, Medicare, Medicaid, and unemployment benefits, could cover cash shortfalls left in household accounts by a fall in private spending. Because such spending is financed with government debt, it also serves the purpose of meeting the demand for safe assets prompted by anxiety about the viability of business debt. Automatic stabilization of incomes also provided automatic stabilization of portfolios:

> One implication of the large increase in government debt and deficits
> that occurred during the recession year of 1975 is that various businesses

and financial institutions were able to acquire safe and secure assets, which improved the liquidity of portfolios, even as aggregate income and employment fell ... . As businesses liquidated inventories, they decreased their indebtedness to banks and acquired government debt. Banks and other financial institutions acquired liquidity by buying government debt rather than by decreasing their assets and liabilities. The public, both households and business, not only acquired safe assets in the form of bank deposits and savings deposits, but were able to decrease their indebtedness relative to income. The existence of a large and increasing government debt thus acted as a significant stabilizer of portfolios during the threatening period of 1975. ([1986e] 2008, 40f.)

Minsky was at pains, however, to emphasize the limits on government spending as a source of cash-flow validation. He views the Treasury as doing the work of a bank – as he does everywhere in his theory of financial capitalism – matching cash inflows with cash outflows. The government is just an economic actor in this regard, and its promises will be judged relative to its ability to meet them:

> To repeat, any organization with large debts outstanding cannot deviate by very much or for very long from at least the promise of a cash flow surplus without having the quality of the debt deteriorate. Any deviation from a government budget that is balanced or in surplus must be understood as transitory – the war will be over, the resource-development program will be finished, or income will be at the full-employment level. ([1986e] 2008, 338)

Government debt could provide the funds to validate problematic private debt, but that debt too, in other words, would require validation, and so the government could not run in deficit forever. Minsky's is a seamless view of capitalism, in which no entity is free from the survival constraint. Even the central bank, the unique entity in Minsky's interpretation, only maintains the power to loosen the survival constraint in the context of its relationships with the rest of the payment system. The fact that the central bank normally transacts in government debt does not mean that it does so mechanically, or that it is obligated to discount all government debt, and so the existence of a central bank cannot be relied on to dismiss theoretically the idea of a survival constraint even for a government with a sovereign currency. This point merits emphasis because the argument is sometimes made, with Minsky cited in support, that the government's power to create money is inherently unlimited, and that therefore there is no financial constraint on government intervention (Lavoie (2013) is both kind and comprehensive in his dismissal of this argument).

Minsky emphatically did not believe that the government faces no survival constraint. The logic of the survival constraint is more primitive, in his analysis, than the institutional structure of central banking or sovereign borrowing:

> Debts embody payment commitments, promises to make payments. For these promises to have value any debtor has to be able to generate a positive cash flow in its favor. It achieves this by operating in the various markets where it buys and sells so as to achieve a cash flow net of operating costs that exceeds the commitments to pay on account of debt. "Has to be able" does not mean does. A unit may have negative cash flows for a considerable period and its liabilities would still be of value because it is accepted that the negative cash flows are transitory. ... A government can run a deficit during a recession without suffering a deterioration of its creditworthiness if there is a tax and spending regime in place that would yield a favorable cash flow (a surplus) under reasonable and attainable circumstances.
>
> There is nothing special about government debt, and a flight from government debt can occur. For a foreign-held debt such a flight will lead to a deterioration of the currency on the exchanges; for a domestic debt the flight can lead to inflation and a need to pay ever higher interest rates to have the debt held. Incidentally, if the central bank – the Federal Reserve – monetizes government debts in order to maintain its nominal price in the face of a deteriorating willingness to hold such debt, then there can be a run from the Federal Reserve as well as from commercial bank liabilities. Just as private business debts have to be validated by profits, as bank liabilities by receipts from assets, as a foreign debt by an export surplus, so government debt has to be validated by an excess of tax receipts over current expenditures. ([1986e] 2008, 336f)

\* \* \*

## Regulation and uncertainty

A consequence of the validation of debt structures is the moral hazard dilemma of the lender of last resort. If lenders know that the central bank will not allow the system to collapse, why should they be prudent in the first place? Help will arrive if things go bad. Institutions can respond strategically by becoming systemically important and thus "too big to fail": if a specific actor knows that its failure will imperil the system, then it can count on the eventual support of the lender of last resort; such an actor can therefore engage in riskier behavior now in anticipation. There is thus a trade-off between prevention and intervention; if the central bank takes a light touch as regulator of banks, it will find itself obliged to act later: "In the 1980s, the attenuation of regulation has been accompanied by an increase in lender of last resort interventions. It is a mistake to equate deregulation with a shift to the market determination of outcomes. Instead, constraint by regulation has been supplanted with protection by refinancing" (1986b, 9).

The problem appears in a subtler guise at a systemic level. The assumption that the central bank will validate the financial structure means that borrowers and lenders will proceed with abandon, economizing more severely on reserves and making the structure more fragile. If a single actor can be prevented from becoming systemically important, then it can be allowed to fail, but the central bank should not allow the system as a whole to fail. Minsky learned this lesson from the experience of 1929: "Perhaps one reason for the great crash was that the private and banking communities believed that there was an implicit contingent liability of the Federal Reserve System in member bank liabilities, whereas the Federal Reserve System, being narrowly legalistic, operated as if no such commitment existed" (1967b, 270). The central bank cannot simply stand by and watch the system crumble, any more than it can give up its discretionary power.

The tension hinges on uncertainty. The validation of debt structures is meaningful only if it is not assured; there is no value to finance if all loans are repaid. Uncertainty is the crux of the central bank's dilemma: distinguished by its position in the payment system, which allows it to force a cash flow in its favor at its discretion, the central bank has a measure of control over this uncertainty. Where most actors must reckon with uncertainty about their ability to pay, the central bank must reckon with its own power to choose. Liquidity, the ability to control the flow of payment on one's initiative, is a precise antidote to this uncertainty.

When financial positions can be entered or exited easily – when markets are liquid, and especially when they are expected to *remain* liquid – then the burden of uncertainty is felt to be light. Private actors can postpone choice, retaining initiative, and "no initiative on [central banks'] part is as a rule called for" (Schumpeter 1939, 657). Yes, perhaps things will change for the worse in the future, but a suitable portfolio adjustment will account for that when the time comes. Assets can be bought and sold, money borrowed and lent, as needed, and what is uncertain now is left to be accommodated later, when the relevant information comes to light. This assumption that liquidity is free, and will always be free, is at the heart of the Walrasian view of the market (Mehrling 2010), though Minsky and Schumpeter recognized that it is an assumption that does not always hold.

Thus the job of the central bank, as the operator of the discretionary element of the financial system, the arbiter of initiative, depends on the manipulation of uncertainty. The too-big-to-fail problem is that certainty comes to prevail, so that the systemically important institution is no longer bound by uncertainty. Minsky suggested that support should be assured for the system as a whole while ensuring that individual actors doubt their own salvation. "This responsibility for the performance of the economy must be carried out in such a way that severe financial losses and distress for any particular unit remain possible" (1964a, 375). This points to, but does not solve, the problem of moral hazard. It assumes that regulation can keep banks from maneuvering into a position where their failure and systemic failure become one and the same. A more mature Minsky accepted defeat: it was "utopian" to imagine shrinking the largest banks (1985c, 18). The existence of the lender of last resort with systemic responsibility reduces uncertainty, and everyone knows it.

Even so, uncertainty might be strategically deployed to counteract the excessive certainty of a boom, as it was in 1966. "The economic significance of the crunch is that a sufficiently high price, both objectively in terms of money cost and subjectively in terms of fear and uncertainty, was extracted from commercial banks, life insurance companies, savings intermediaries and non-financial corporations so that in 1967, [they] preferred more conservative portfolios than they accepted in 1966" (1968b, 79; also 1968c). In a boom, a dangerous unanimity arises – it becomes hard to imagine that the boom will come to an end, and so speculation is overdone. Borrowers can be nudged back into more conservative positions by making money a bit harder to come by, and at the same time leaving open the question of their survival.

Such tactics might succeed over the course of a single cycle, but still fail over a longer horizon. Though the particular excesses of an expansion can be curbed, each cycle leaves a legacy of validated commitments that sets the stage for renewed speculation. "Each time an embryonic financial crisis is prevented from escalation by Federal Reserve intervention, the rate of inflation [moves] to a higher plateau" (1974d, 34). The actions of a lender of last resort, that is, cannot be reduced to a simple rule. "Only in times of stagnation or tranquillity [*sic*] can the economy afford a central bank that stands on principle" (1967a, 55).

# 7

# *The resilience of economics*

## Anticipation of crisis

We are ten years on from the global financial crisis of 2008. It is enough history to create a barrier to communication between those of us who had reached socially aware adulthood by then, such as myself, and those who had not, like my students. It is not enough time, though, for the crisis to have been definitively named – Global Financial Crisis is bland and not entirely distinctive, while Subprime Crisis seems not to convey the scope or scale of the event, which encompassed not only that small segment of the US housing finance market, but many of the central institutions of the US and international financial system itself. Perhaps the political, social, and intellectual reverberations of the crisis have not quietened sufficiently to allow reflection.

Crisis is recognizable as a discrete, acute disruption. A systemic financial crisis seems to erupt suddenly, quickly spreading to envelop the entire system. Minsky was at pains to argue that crisis arises out of the normal functioning of a capitalist economy – it is not a moment when the rules are inapplicable; it is a moment when the structure of the system is most clearly in evidence, as it unravels. This book begins from that point, as Minsky did, both in the content of his argument – outlining a theory of capitalism for normal times no less than crisis times – and in his rhetorical thrusts – using each crisis as an opportunity to call attention to the developing argument, to build an audience, to try to win over colleagues.

Minsky's is a theory of capitalism as a system, with acute events as the extreme implications of its basic principles. At the most primitive level, it is a theory about the survival constraint, the point when a single actor's next payment is in question; at its most expansive, it is about crisis, when the entire payment system is in question. The survival constraint is in effect at every moment – for the cornerstone of the market is that one must pay one's debts – yet not every default becomes a crisis. The subprime crisis is our most recent systemic disruption – September 15, 2008, the date of Lehman's bankruptcy and the day before AIG received emergency funding, if one had to pick a single day.

This chapter is oriented around that point in time, that particular moment in the timeline of capitalism. We take up a single question – "what is crisis to capitalism?" – from three perspectives in time, in each of three sections: before, during, and after. First, in this section, before.

Reflecting back on his pre-crisis views, the CEO of monoline insurer ACA, which had written tens of billions of dollars' worth of credit-default swaps on CDOs, said to his staff:

> We never expected losses. … We were providing hedges on market volatility to institutional counterparties. … We were positioned, we believed, to take the volatility because we didn't have to post collateral against the changes in market value to our counterparty, number one. Number two, we were told by the rating agencies that rated us that that mark-to-market variation was not important to our rating. (FCIC 2011, 276f.)

This constellation of beliefs certainly looks audacious in hindsight: the insurer's large clients would never take on gambles they could not handle; the company would be somehow insulated from the systemic potential of collateral calls and mark-to-market require- ments. One might simply label such behavior as hubris, and set out to regulate it away. Capitalism can be saved from its own essential flaw (the argument would go), its tendency toward fragility, by the identification and containment of risky behavior.

ACA was in fine company in its sanguine expectations; much of the expansion in the market-based credit system was driven by similar views. But this should not be understood as a failure of analytical rigor, a lack of due diligence on the part of individual actors. The same expectations were embedded in the most elaborate and technical of assessments. In setting aside reserves against their securitization holdings, for example, banks could use their own models to establish an estimate of losses for the purposes of computing the capital charge. "Citigroup judged that the capital requirement for the super-senior tranches of synthetic CDOs it held for trading purposes was effectively zero, because the prices didn't move much" (FCIC 2011, 196f.). Asked to anticipate how they would make position when, one day, the survival constraint might bind, the bank responded that there was no possibility that it would do so.

The same logic finds other expression. Writing about the repo markets, the FCIC notes that "[t]he short-term nature of repo money also makes it inherently risky and unreliable: funding that is offered at certain terms today could be gone tomorrow. ... Yet more and more, repo lenders were loaning money to funds ... rolling the debt nightly, and not worrying very much about the real quality of the collateral" (FCIC 2011, 136). The repo market was structured around a payment commitment that would bind over and over; observing that the daily survival constraint was rarely binding, and easily met by refinance, the collateral seemed not to enter very much into the calculation. The underlying securities were the basis for this repo finance, which facilitated the issuance and holding of those securities and so the expansion of the securities-based banking system. Like all securities, they embodied payment commitments, derived for example from mortgage securitizations, and the value of collateral was, in theory, that those commitments might form the basis of a position-making effort should the repo borrower default. The collateral might be sold, or its owner might simply collect the mortgage payments. As with ACA and Citigroup, even the most professional of borrowers and lenders could not foresee the potential for collapse. "'The repo market, I mean it functioned fine up until one day it just didn't function,' [hedge fund manager Ralph] Cioffi told the FCIC" (FCIC 2011, 136).

After the fact, the temptation is to suppose that the dangers should have been visible, that everyone should have known. The participants had the tools to anticipate those risks; funding markets had seized up in the past. But this misses the point. The FCIC's blithe assessment about repo, like many post hoc opinions, that such markets were risky is in reality a statement that they eventually failed. Risk, in this argument, is something that was always present because it eventually manifested. It is true: short-term funding can be here today and gone tomorrow. Yes, if borrowers and lenders and regulators had behaved differently, the subsequent events would have played out differently.

The problem with such arguments is they imagine a way out, where in fact there is none. The imagined way out is that that the risks come from without and can therefore be anticipated and avoided. We know the liquidity risks, the rollover risks, inherent in short-term funding and so can reduce our reliance on them. We know that default is a possibility and so can require provisions for position-making. We are aware that liquidity is valuable and so can constrain the economization on reserves to within bounds, and prevent it from being overdone. These anticipations, however, can only be reactive to an underlying structure that they do nothing to change. They are a version of Goodhart's Law: "[A]ny observed statistical regularity will tend to collapse once pressure is placed upon it for control purposes" (Goodhart 1984, 96). Greater prudence now might mean that payment is more easily made at some future moment, but it makes the survival constraint harder to meet now. It is a way of trying to make liquidity valuable, against a systemic configuration that says it is not.

The risk does not come from without; it comes from within the very constitution of financial capitalism. The survival constraint is nothing but the requirement to pay; to economize on reserves is nothing but a way to try to loosen that constraint in the future. The result, crisis, is a flaw of capitalism, but it is not abnormal. The flaw is essential; it is an expression of the logic of capitalism itself. An anticipated crisis is not a crisis, but Minsky's central point is that crisis is inevitable, that financial patterns cultivated in periods of prosperity are precisely those that lead to eventual disruption. It is not just that the possibility of financial crisis is discounted; it must be that it is systematically excluded from anticipation.

Crisis evades the capitalist imagination, though certainly some individuals do manage to imagine it, perhaps even quite precisely. But their anticipation is not enough to forestall the crash; it cannot be. Those who could see were not in a position to act; those who were in a position to act did not see, or could not or would not act. Anticipation of the crisis and action in response to anticipation are divorced.

The flaw of financial capitalism, Minsky made clear, is its instability, an inevitable consequence of the survival constraint and the behaviors that follow from it. Minsky believed that the flaw was essential to the workings of capitalism, and so inescapable: even with enlightened theory, regulation, and central-bank practice, crisis could not be avoided entirely. Put another way, though capitalism is flawed, the task is not to eliminate that flaw as though it is a wound that can be healed. "I am afraid economists can never become mere technicians applying an agreed-upon theory that is fit for all seasons within an institutional structure that does not and need not change" (1978d, 21).

\* \* \*

The 2008 crisis gave rise to renewed interest in Minsky's ideas, and rightly so. The preceding chapters have elaborated his theory of capitalism, a theory with financial concerns – with payment – as a central, foundational element. They have also followed the sequential development of his thought, using his major projects as milestones by which to give some shape to an intellectual process that was inevitably organic and incremental. I have tried, in these two threads, to show what Minsky knew, and at the same time, in parallel, how he knew it.

Hyman Minsky died in 1996, and so we are left to formulate our own observations about the events of 2008. As the names of Simons, Schumpeter, and Keynes resonated for Minsky, so Minsky's name resonates after the 2008 crisis. Minsky found his way of being an economist, using texts and unfolding history as sources, each one held up against a maintained theory, and each one providing some new ingredient for the next iteration of that theory. He took the legacy of those authors and held fast to the study of capitalism. It is a mistake to offer predictions about the future of capitalism and the impending next crisis. Rather, I ask this question: what is our way of knowing Minsky? Texts and history require interpretation, which derives from what has gone before and informs what comes next. Minsky's texts, and the events surrounding the crisis of 2008, become our own texts, our own unfolding history, the basis for our own interpretation.

Up to a certain point, interpretations of Minsky largely agree: the catchphrases "stability is destabilizing" and "hedge, speculative, Ponzi" are sufficiently full of meaning that they serve to communicate the message almost on their own. So far as they go, these slogans are well chosen, because they do seem to get across something about what Minsky had to say. Yet each author gives their own elaboration, as I have given mine, and within the bounds of these slogans, the interpreters vary. Each is something of a translator, rendering a part of Minsky's thought in their own theoretical language. In holding these translations side by side, it becomes clear that we who in our different ways study the financial system do not always give the same meanings to the same words. Our translations of Minsky, as such, are not only more and less faithful, but also to a degree incompatible. In what follows here and in the next two sections I ask about three ideas, all central to Minsky, that are subject to differing interpretations: time, loss, and liquidity.

To begin: Minsky's world is set definitively in time. His first principle, the survival constraint, defines a particular point in time, that moment at which a debt comes due, and divides the rest of history into a period before and a period after. Before the debt comes due, the borrower experiences anxiety about the possibility that funds will not be available, responding with position-making, following those channels that seem like plausible sources of funds. Urgency increases as the moment approaches. At the moment of payment, a discrete and known instant in time, the payment is either made or not made. Afterwards, there is survival or failure but not doubt.

Crisis is a similar narrative, told in an aggregate setting. One difference that results is that, although individual debts are due at known points in time, the arrival time of systemic crisis is not known in advance, at least not with certainty. As I have done in my own version, every reteller of Minsky's story has some way of getting from the individual level to the systemic level, which must, at least implicitly, address this difference. There must be a way that the crisis is delayed, until finally it cannot be put back any longer. Auerback, McCulley, and Parenteau, for example, put the prices of capital assets and financial assets center-stage. It is rising asset prices that validate, not financial structures as in this volume, but instead the behavior these embody:

> As more and more agents progress from hedge to speculative to Ponzi units, their purchasing power goes up. More goods and services are produced and purchased, and prices of existing tangible and financial assets are bid up. As cash flows to households and businesses beat expectations, the very act of moving from one stage to the next drives up asset prices and therefore validates the risk seeking behavior. In a sense, rising asset prices cover all sins. (Auerback, McCulley, and Parenteau 2010, 120)

It is a cycle based on asset prices, where less conservative attitudes toward cash flows push prices up. Perhaps by the sale of these assets, cash inflows rise, fueling the behavior. Lavoie likewise emphasizes the structured, cyclical character of financial fragility, with one phase of the cycle connected to the next by behavioral regularities in place of asset prices. In such a reading, the defining element of the theory is its repetitive cyclicality; one phase of the cycle gives way to the next in a pattern that can be anticipated:

> Minsky asserts that households, firms and banks are willing to adopt more risky behaviour and strategies in periods of economic boom or after a long period of high growth. Minsky argues that in such situations banks ease their risk premia as well as their lending criteria, accepting higher debt loads ... In addition, all agents – that is households, firms and banks – will willingly hold smaller proportions of less liquid assets. This is the paradox of tranquillity: stability breeds instability. A period of relative stability and high economic activity will eventually lead to more fragile financial conditions. More speculative behaviour will also accompany greater financial fragility. Indeed, firms and banks will compete against one another using debt as a lever; households will soon follow suit ... Eventually, the central bank will weigh in and impose credit constraints ... Given the higher debt loads, higher rates of interest will further erode the fragility of the system making it more difficult to meet the interest payments on existing debt. At this point, banks will surely change their behaviour by tightening both their risk premia and their lending criteria. All this may translate into a stock market crash, unless governments stand ready to support aggregate demand. (Lavoie 2006, 72f.)

In Lavoie's telling, each stage of the cycle has its characteristic behaviors, formulaic like a soap opera, with the dramatic finale visible well in advance. The succession of attitudes toward risk and the prevalence of adventurous lending move the plot forward. Mehrling, by contrast, who invokes Minsky in addressing the Fed's response to the 2008 crisis, focuses on refinance as the mechanism connecting one moment to the next: when the survival constraint binds, the question is whether there will be a lender to push it back another day. Fragility amounts to an increasing reliance on the refinance mechanism: more actors who need to roll over debts at any given moment, and therefore also more actors who will face default when the refinance mechanism breaks down:

> For Minsky, the inherent instability of credit is all about the shifting balance between cash commitments and cash flows. "Hedge" finance structures, in which promised future cash commitments are always less than realized cash inflows, are inherently stable; a business financed in such a way can never run into liquidity problems and therefore can focus its attention on other matters. The problem is that, over time,

hedge structures tend to be replaced by speculative and then Ponzi finance structures, in which firms promise payments that they cannot necessarily meet from concurrent cash flow. In good times, these more fragile finance structures cause no trouble; when the promised debts come due, they are just rolled over to a future date. But the fragility is there nonetheless, since any dislocation in the refinance mechanism can cause disruption. When the dislocation comes, the size of the resulting disruption depends on the prevalence of speculative and Ponzi finance structures that are vulnerable to such a dislocation. (Mehrling 2010, 68)

Refinance in Mehrling is quite synonymous with position-making: refinance is the need, to delay the day of reckoning, and position-making emphasizes that borrowers are not random in their search: they have recourse to specific markets and mechanisms according to convention and general practice. The past is the source of the commitments that are maturing today, and refinance is the hope for postponing those binding commitments from the present into the future. Validation enters in an essential way in such a telling, because each successful refinance, each validation of an outstanding debt structure, delays but does not remove the survival constraint; only changes in the underlying activity, that which gives rise to the cash commitments in the first place, can do so. Minsky's sense of time is an essential part of Mehrling's analytical frame, for "[t]he economics view and the finance view meet in the present, where cash flows emerging from past real investments meet cash commitments entered into in anticipation of an imagined future. This present is the natural sphere of the *money* view" (Mehrling 2010, 4).

Time measured by price; time as cycle; time as delay. Minsky's theory is nothing without time, but here are three quite different translations of that term, with different nuances and suggesting something different about the nature of what Minsky was describing.

\* \* \*

# Breaking point

The high point of a financial crisis is recognizable by the apparent vulnerability of core institutions to failure: in September 2008, Lehman Brothers failed, the second of the major investment banks to do so (after Bear Stearns earlier that year); the massive insurance company AIG required government support; and the government-sponsored mortgage lenders Fannie Mae and Freddie Mac were close to collapse. Each of these institutions was experiencing, at that moment, a sharply binding survival constraint; in the event the source of the binding constraint was mortgage credit, and securitizations and derivatives based on mortgage credit. The crisis was systemic, however, not because of the nature of the commitments or even because of their scale, but rather because the possibility had become real that they would not be met, and that the failure of large institutions would entail the failure of the system itself.

In his early work, Minsky was careful to train his focus on systemic fragility, on the system's vulnerability to crisis; the particular industries or practices that gave rise to the vulnerability being of secondary importance. In a fragile system, with highly articulated patterns of cash commitments, even a small event, one that would not have great repercussions in normal times, could have systemic consequences. Thus the underlying conditions in the US housing market, which had prompted warnings for several years, or the patterns of securitization, which had developed over decades, were relevant for the crisis of 2008 only as they gave rise to systemic vulnerability.

Such vulnerability is a consequence of the rules of the game. The prosperity that reigns in normal times, like that which preceded the crisis of 2008, is what gives rise to the collapse. At that break, the critical moment, it is the intervention of a lender of last resort that loosens the survival constraint for those core institutions whose continued existence constitutes the continued existence of the system itself. The fundamental requirement of capitalism, that one must pay one's debts, is in that instant weakened, just enough to allow the normal operation of the system to resume. For that instant the survival constraint is lifted, not for everyone but for the top of the hierarchy, just long enough to relieve the systemic threat.

Such suspension is by no means an exception particular to 2008; it is a part of the script for crisis. In the Panic of 1825, famously, "'[w]e lent [money],' said Mr. Harman, on behalf of the Bank of England, 'by every possible means and in modes we had never adopted before'" (Bagehot 1873, ch. II, s. II, par. 12). Following much the same script, in 2008 the Federal Reserve extended a trillion dollars of lending in a matter of weeks using a range of newly created facilities (TAF, TSLF, PDCF, CPFF, and others) (Grad, Mehrling, and Neilson 2011). The nature of those facilities, activated at the breaking point of crisis, reveals the structures that had been assembled in the boom that went before it: they brought credit to the securities dealing system, to support repo and commercial paper markets, and eventually to absorb much of the money markets onto the Fed's balance sheet. It was only in their resort to public support, to the operator of the discretionary element of the economy, that we learned about the patterns of payment commitments that had been cemented, over the preceding years, in the market-based credit system.

It is no accident that official intervention coincides with the point at which the survival constraint binds at the core of the system. When a default occurs – when a promised payment is not made – at the individual level, it calls into question the viability of the actor in distress. But when core institutions are on the brink, when the survival of central, infrastructural actors is in doubt, it calls into question the viability of all promised payments, of the system as a whole. The rules of the game must be bent, the requirement to pay loosened, because the issue has become existential. "[A]t the apex where the very survival of the system is at stake, law tends to be more elastic by design and/or because the system's ultimate backstop abrogates the discretionary power to do what it takes to rescue the system" (Pistor 2013, 320). When the system's survival is tantamount to the survival of key institutions, the systemic actors can and do change the rules to save the system.

Systemic actors, those at the core, feel the threat to their own survival. But because these infrastructural institutions are private entities, intervention out of public resources – bailout – must be justified. The threat of failure must be widely agreed to be systemic, and the fear of failure widely felt. In the effort to obtain the approval of the US Congress for the Treasury's $700 billion Troubled Asset Relief Program (TARP), an attempt to restore the normal functioning of the financial system, the then Fed Chair Ben Bernanke offered unrestrained metaphors, telling

the Joint Economic Committee Wednesday [September 24, 2008]: "…
I think it is extraordinarily important to understand that … choking up of credit is like taking the lifeblood away from the economy." He told the House Financial Services Committee on the same day, "People are saying, 'Wall Street, what does it have to do with me?' That is the way they are thinking about it. Unfortunately, it has a lot to do with them. It will affect their company, it will affect their job, it will affect their economy. That affects their own lives, affects their ability to borrow and to save and to save for retirement and so on." By the evening of Sunday, September 28, as bankers and regulators

hammered out Wachovia's rescue, congressional negotiators had agreed on the outlines of a deal. (FCIC 2011, 372)

The core institutions knew that their survival was on the line, and Bernanke's argument was that everyone else's survival was, too.

Notably, the Fed's interventions in 2008, aiding not only US banks but also US securities dealers, and foreign banks via their central banks, was an answer to a question Minsky had earlier asked. He had noted that the Fed's intervention in support of offshore dollar banking during the Franklin National crisis confirmed its role as international lender of last resort. Surely this was on his mind when he asked, a decade later:

> The emergence and internationalization of securitized financial instruments, together with the continued growth of offshore banks, means that there is a vast pool of dollar-denominated and other currency-denominated assets which lies outside the formal domain of responsibility of the Federal Reserve or of any other central bank. The question of who is the "They" that will act as lenders of last resort for securitized assets and offshore banks remains entirely open. (1986b, 14)

At the break, we learned that the Fed was the "they" who would act: the crisis was understood, was felt to be existential; someone had to act, and only the US Federal Reserve could loosen the survival constraint for the actors in trouble, not only in its own jurisdiction but everywhere.

\* \* \*

Just as Minsky's is a narrative set in time, so it is a story of loss. The entrepreneur takes on an uncertain venture, borrowing to do so and promising to repay based on hopes for the venture's success. There would be no story if the possibility of loss were not real: the venture must be truly uncertain, so that the entrepreneur's promises are indeed contingent. As the borrower acts in spite of this uncertainty, so they must convince their lender to do the same. The lender, in turn, faces their own possibility of loss. The survival constraint, then, is the moment of truth, when the venture's success is revealed – at least for now. Disaster is put off, for borrower and lender alike.

The narrative is premised on the possibility of loss, and attitudes toward that possibility often figure prominently. The possibility of loss goes by two names in economics, made familiar by Frank Knight (1921): risk and uncertainty. Both are assessments of the future, and both emphasize the lack of knowledge. Keynes made uncertainty a pivotal part of *The General Theory*, illustrating the distinction by comparing the outcome of a turn of a roulette wheel – which we can call risk – with the prospect of war – which we can call uncertainty. Risk, in this line of thinking, is the possibility of loss that is quantifiable or definite in some way. Uncertainty, by contrast, encapsulates the more ineffable quality of the future, around which bounds cannot be readily established, and in the face of which statistics, the mathematical treatment of risk, is of little help.

It is risk, not uncertainty, that makes more frequent appearance in paraphrases of Minsky's story. For Sheila Dow, it is the changing perception of risk that provokes an upswing:

> For Minsky, boom periods result from a growing tendency to reduce expectation of risk and to expect an increasing appreciation of asset values, with consequent growth in credit and thus exposure to risk. This tendency increases the fragility of the financial system and thus its potential for reversals, as expectations are confounded and defaults increase. (Dow 2010, 246)

Risk here has an existence outside of the behavior of actors in the financial system: they form quantifiable expectations about loss, which give rise to a boom as those quantities diminish. Those expectations are a misperception, however, and the same behavior that leads to the boom leads actors to unknowingly expose themselves to greater possibility of loss. The perceptual gap is finally closed when risk reappears. (It must be said that Dow has elsewhere done much to emphasize fundamental uncertainty; here I am simply noting her characterization of Minsky in terms of quantifiable risk (Dow 2012).) Steve Keen, whose writing both before and after the 2008 crisis has sought relentlessly to turn the economics profession's attention to Minsky (Keen 2011; Keen 2017), deals not with perceptions of risk but with the price charged for bearing it, the risk premium:

> Two things gradually become evident to managers and bankers: "Existing debts are easily validated and units that were heavily in debt prospered: it paid to lever" [1982b, 65]. As a result, both managers and bankers come to regard the previously accepted risk premium as excessive. Investment projects are evaluated using less conservative estimates of prospective cash flows, so that with these rising expectations go rising investment and asset prices. The general decline in risk aversion thus sets off both growth in investment and exponential

growth in the price level of assets, which is the foundation of both the boom and its eventual collapse. (Keen 1995 611; Keen 2011)

In Keen's version, the memory of a past crisis means that risk premia are high, and so only low-risk ventures are undertaken. Growth results, ventures are successful, and the price of risk falls. The price reflects not necessarily a perception of risk but a willingness to bear it, and that willingness sustains a general boom. Risk here appears as something external to the process, a condition of business activity that is known and knowable, but whose price rises and falls with the willingness to bear it. In this sense, Wray's reading is much the same, placing risk and attitudes toward risk at the center of the story. "During an upswing, profit-seeking firms and banks become more optimistic, taking on riskier financial structures. Firms commit larger portions of expected revenues to debt service. Lenders accept smaller down payments and lower quality collateral" (Wray 2016, 31).

These narratives suppose that the relevant possibilities of loss are quantifiable, in the form of an expected loss or in the form of a price for bearing that loss. Though such quantifications may be imperfect, they can be known: they are much more risk than uncertainty. Risk arises in these stories of financial instability, moreover, as an external factor, something outside of the financial system, about which those quantifications are formed.

The opposite approaches surely present a rockier path. To ask after uncertainty, the more truly unknowable aspect of the future, is to put aside the analytical conventions and efficacy of statistics, avoiding even their implicit use. If existence is beset with uncertainty, rather than risk, the problems of what we do not know are that much more intractable. But it must be down that path – the uncertain one, not the risky one – that Minsky's theory leads us. A risky venture may fail, to be sure. But where the possibility of loss is quantifiable, where a venture can lead only to a future that though not fully known is delimited and quantifiable, then failure is contained, and the systemic, existential possibility of crisis is absent.

That existential contingency is the central thrust of Minsky's analysis of crisis, which is trenchant precisely insofar as it shows that capitalism's instability follows from its very foundations: the requirement to pay when due. The possibility of loss that most requires attention, that is, is the possibility of systemic loss, the loss that manifests as the price paid for the survival of the system itself. Systemic crisis, for Minsky, is a consequence of factors internal to the structure of capitalism itself, not an external phenomenon. Intrinsic uncertainty, not extrinsic risk, is the problem, one that cannot be easily expressed in the mathematical language preferred by today's economists.

\* \* \*

## Memory of crisis

Each crisis, for Minsky, was evidence of the failure of prevailing economic theory, and new evidence in favor of his own. The fact that the mounting evidence did not have much effect on the state of economic theory was a source of frustration. How could actual repeated examples of instability simply not count as evidence against a theory that denied their very possibility? This question has echoes after the 2008 crisis:

> Following the financial crisis of 2007–8, many progressive academics and commentators loudly declared that the event was simply the manifestation of what they had long argued – namely, that rampant speculation in unregulated financial markets was felling an unstable accumulation of financial claims entirely out of balance with fundamental values, and that this would sooner or later lead to a massive crisis. (Konings 2018, 1)

Neither the ultimate breakdown of capitalism, nor a sea change in economic theory, have resulted from the crisis of 2008. It is not that there has been no reflection: the mechanics of the market-based credit system that came to light in their unraveling have certainly come under scrutiny. "In theory, securitization, over-the-counter derivatives and the many byways of the shadow banking system were supposed to distribute risk efficiently among investors. The theory would prove to be wrong" (FCIC 2011, 212). Far from an efficient distribution of losses, they would turn out to be concentrated at the core of the financial system.

But what lesson should be learned from 2008? A post-crisis, pre-crisis period is when the lessons of the last crisis are incorporated. Minsky worried about a Maginot line mentality: safeguards in the financial system, as well as developments in economic theory, would respond to the specifics of the last crisis. Meanwhile, financial practices would continue to evolve, in response to the ever-present urgency of the survival constraint. The next crisis would be different, exposing new vulnerabilities among practices, markets, and institutions.

Minsky's thought, taken as a whole, does give some help in this regard, as I hope I have demonstrated in the preceding chapters. For what is new in finance is not completely new; the logic of payment compels a set of behaviors that can be described efficiently using Minsky's language. The survival constraint, the requirement to pay, is the most basic principle, and from it follow the need to make position and the desire to economize on cash. This gives rise to a central place for liquidity, and so also a central place for the behavior of market-making activity. What is essential for market-making is initiative, whence the special status of the central bank.

Minsky made great use of these ideas over several inter-crisis periods, refining them and putting them to work on each new set of circumstances. But he had concluded early on that financial capitalism was inherently unstable, and so, although he might have been frustrated that he did not make more converts, he was never too surprised. There will always be another crisis in a system based on payment; efforts to restrain financial excess can divert the need to make payment but cannot eliminate it. When instability arises again in the network of payment commitments, it will not appear right in front of our eyes. The next crisis will not be totally different; it will be just different enough to slip through.

\* \* \*

Minsky's story plays out over time; present at all times is the possibility of loss. With their behavior constrained by the requirement to pay, actors must be attentive to their sources of the means of payment. Thus, as already argued, the central place for liquidity in Minsky's work. Faced with the survival constraint, actors need to make position, and liquidity describes their ability to do so. If actors are liquid, they can readily command cash flows; if the market for a particular security is liquid, it can readily be exchanged for cash.

It is hard to talk about liquidity without a theory of market-making, yet this is what economists, with notable exceptions, have had to do. The Walrasian conception, that supply and demand confront one another directly, in various metaphorical forms – auction, barter, recontract – leaves no room for the intervention of dealers. Real markets, however, do not exist but for the efforts of market-makers. By buying from sellers and selling to buyers, it is market-makers that create liquidity, that create the possibility of transacting. Crisis is the moment when the survival constraint seems to bind everywhere at once, when cash cannot be raised by selling or borrowing, when it is impossible to transact at any price, and thus it is just the moment when liquidity vanishes. A theory of markets that does not account for the origins of liquidity can say little about its disappearance.

Without a theory of market-making, liquidity finds expression in other ways in the retellings of Minsky. In the moment of panic, the pressure is in general to sell assets to make position, and so the idea of the press for cash can manifest as a falling price. Just so in Dow's version:

> A key element of the process is that illiquidity problems, through knock-on effects on assets valuation, can create insolvency problems. ... While uncertainty diminishes with the general confidence in low risk during the boom period, the reversal increases uncertainty about future asset values, encouraging a rise in liquidity preference which continues as expectations become more firmly held of asset price deflation. (Dow 2010, 246)

Uncertainty, that is, leads to a search for liquidity, which makes its effect felt in falling prices that then, perhaps through mark-to-market requirements, render institutions insolvent. Insolvency, the excess of liabilities over assets, is the test for survival here, not liquidity, the ability to pay. In Keen's version, similarly, illiquidity is felt through prices.

> Such businesses will find themselves having to sell assets to finance their debt servicing – and this entry of new sellers into the market for assets pricks the exponential growth of asset prices. With the price boom checked, Ponzi financiers now find themselves with assets that can no longer be traded at a profit, and levels of debt that cannot be serviced from the cash flows of the businesses they now control. Banks that financed these asset purchases now find that their leading customers can no longer pay their debts – and this realization leads initially to a further bank-driven increase in interest rates. Liquidity is suddenly much more highly prized; holders of illiquid assets attempt to sell them in return for liquidity. The asset market becomes flooded and the euphoria becomes a panic, the boom becomes a slump. (Keen 1995, 612f.; Keen 2011, 329)

An excess of sellers pushes prices down, and it is falling prices that impair balance sheets (as in Dow's version) and make payment impossible. Illiquid markets, that is, cause insolvency, which causes payment failures. There are no market-makers in such an account, and so although liquidity is highly prized, that view finds no behavioral expression. Mehrling's encapsulation, by contrast, written before 2008 but after a thorough reading of Minsky's work (Mehrling 1999), shows the connection from individual liquidity problems to systemic liquidity problems and systemic crisis:

> At the aggregate level, the natural upward instability of the system leaves behind a residue of financial commitments that pose problems for the continuation of growth. At the individual level, these problems take the form of a sharply binding survival constraint that forces distressed units to reduce expenditure, sell assets, and/or borrow at high interest rates, all in order to raise cash to meet immediate commitments. At the level of the market, the problems of individuals are reflected in conditions in the money market, which means at the very least a high price of refinance, and at worst a disruption and even breakdown of exchange. If the money market is the heart of the system, then financial crisis is a heart attack. (Mehrling 2000, 83)

Here financial commitments and the survival constraint that they entail are at the center. The survival constraint forces position-making (reduction of expenditure, sale of assets, necessitous borrowing). The individual survival constraint is transmitted by position-making to others, at a price. But the markets for refinance can break down – liquidity crisis. This is supported by a theory of liquidity much like the one that underlies the present volume, made most explicit in (Mehrling 2010, 92–112).

Liquidity was a tricky topic for Minsky, as argued earlier, and it has been a tricky subject for his interpreters. The problem is not incidental: in financial crisis, exchange itself grinds to a halt in the absence of liquidity. In crisis there is no price that will induce buyers to enter the market. This must be because of uncertainty, not risk: if the unknown future could be contained, then a price could be set and markets would open. Answers to these questions, and the interpretation of Minsky, require a theory of market-making.

\* \* \*

# 8

## *Minsky for all moments*

### Financialization

The end of the twentieth century seemed to justify optimism about the stability of the financial system, experience sustaining the belief that while disruptions might still come around, modern central banking and economic theory would allow them to be managed without undue cost to wider society. The experience of 2008 left a dent in that conviction. Yet the crisis has not led to the collapse of capitalism, nor has it torn down the economic theory that serves as capitalism's intellectual scaffolding (Konings 2018). Those who looked at the global financial crisis and saw the end of a capitalism driven by money managers have so far been proven mistaken.

One vector for current critiques of capitalism is to object to financialization. The infiltration of the market, the ever greater prevalence of such market mechanisms in areas of life that were once organized otherwise, is in this view a turn away from the appropriate sphere of the market, and compromises its ability to serve as a beneficial sphere of social existence. As time progressed, Minsky came to share something of this objection. His reference point was always to the post-war years of his early career, and a perhaps idealized picture of entrepreneurial capitalism with a significant role for the state. This had been lost as American corporations shifted "from production to marketing to finance": "The current Wall Street plays indicate that the corporate form has degenerated to the point where it no longer is a reliable engine of progress" (1985e, 60). Writing on October 22, 1987, the week of the Black Monday stock market crash:

"Speculation is not only an enemy of enterprise but also by piling on debt it can set the stage for serious recession" (1987b, A35); at the same time the growth of finance was arrogating the role of the state (1987d).

Responding from his Minskyian point of view to current critics of financialization, not to defend financialization but rather, critically, to suggest that those who object have missed the point, Mehrling offers that "the commitments we make to one another to perform in various ways in the future form the very fabric of the society in which we live. Marriage is like that, and so is credit" (Mehrling 2017, 8). Commitments to pay are not destroying society, they are constitutive of society. Market society, by this argument, is just society, and to study the modalities of finance, as Mehrling does, is to study society itself.

I have at many points followed Mehrling's lead, in this volume and elsewhere, but this view is mistaken: financial commitments cannot be the substance of society. We might note that modern finance is predicated on the transferability of obligations, that there is not much significance to the identity of one's creditors or debtors. If a household mortgage is sold to another bank, then one submits the payment to a different address, but little more has changed than that. Likewise, the choice of one bank over another is of little importance to the depositor, apart from some reassurances about each bank's financial health. Indeed the existence of deposit insurance and bank regulation can be understood as a mechanism by which to ensure that such relationships are functionally anonymous, so that the smooth operation of financial society is assured.

Such anonymity is implicit in the nature of the obligation to pay. Fulfillment of one's social commitments, in this view, is about completing payment, and this is so even if the identity of the lender has changed. It is anonymous credit, where it is the system as a whole that imposes compliance, rather than any quality of the creditor–debtor relationship itself. That anonymity is largely symmetrical: the survival constraint binds for every actor – though, as we have seen, those at the core have greater capacity to loosen it. Even at the very center of all such financial relationships, the central bank is bound in its own way by its centrality. The obligation to pay, separated from the identity of borrower or lender, holds it all together.

Marriage, *contra* Mehrling, is a quite different kind of thing, as are the relationship between parent and child, between student and

teacher, between colleagues, and so on. The commitments we make
to one another in such relationships are anything but anonymous.
My commitments to my children cannot be satisfied by the substitution of parenting commitments from some other comparable
individual. My filial duties cannot be fulfilled on my behalf by an
anonymous third party. My responsibilities to my students cannot
be auctioned off. In all cases, the commitment is not separable from
the individual.

It is *these* commitments, made mutually in the context of
relationships that are inevitably non-anonymous, that form the
very fabric of the society in which we live. They provide the
content of human experience, and thus memory and meaning.
Admittedly, the financial system, the requirement that our debts
be settled in money, and the processes that animate them are infrastructural features that go some way to maintaining the coherence
of financial capitalism over time. Yes, understanding the implications of the survival constraint will be an indispensable guide to
understanding the stability of that system. All this is the premise
of this book. But to say that these features are themselves constitutive of society is to mistake the appearance of the thing for its
substance.

Mechanisms do exist, of course, to enable certain substitutions
in relational situations – adoption, for example, or substitute
teachers – but these are not counterevidence. The relational and
emotional complexity of adoption for all involved, the storied lack
of authority commanded by the substitute teacher, are testaments
precisely to the hefty underlying substance of the relationships
involved, which are not transferable, as credit obligations are. It
is even possible – catnip for economists of a certain stripe – to use
market mechanisms to arrange some such functions: adoption
markets, cash for grades, and so on. One might add organ
markets, prisons, human trafficking, and slavery. In all these
cases, the reason for adding a market mechanism is precisely to
substitute the survival constraint for relational commitments. (I
am trying here to point out a path, not yet clearly illuminated,
from Minsky's understanding of finance to those thinkers who
held fast to the necessity of relation in the face of the dehuman-
izing force of capital (Moten and Harney 2010; Glissant 1997).
This is my path and not Minsky's, so for now I wish just to
acknowledge the debt.)

One might make this argument out to be simply an objection to
financialization: market relationships displace other relationships,

and society is thus impoverished. I do think there is an element of truth to this. Every good teacher whom I have met or studied knows that what matters is the student–teacher relationship (for example, hooks 1994; Yanoshak 2011); the more present the market is in the classroom, the more the relationship is imperiled, at the cost of learning. Not least among such concerns, it seems profoundly inegalitarian to suppose that it is fair to use the market to allocate relationships, that a greater share of society should be enjoyed by those who can pay. It is worth taking note when our ability to relate to one another is compromised by market logic, and to resist this financialization where we can.

There is a deeper critique here, however, one that to my mind follows directly from the theory of the preceding chapters, though I cannot be sure that Minsky reached the same conclusion as I have. Financial capitalism – and all capitalism – is, as Minsky said, essentially financial: it begins from the commitment to make payment when due. Financialization, as Mehrling says, is the increasing substitution of financial relationships for all other relationships, of commitments to pay for all other commitments. Such commitments are enforceable but generic: they exist in the absence of any human qualities of the two parties. They are not only anonymous but in a way one-sided: to borrow, in thoroughgoing financial capitalism, is more a commitment to capitalism, to payment in general, than it is to any particular lender.

Thus this is not an objection to financialization *per se*: it is not resentment of the encroachment of market logic, or nostalgia for times less pervaded by it. The issue is not with the growth or the extent of market logic, but with market logic itself. Such logic is the foundation of Minsky's theory, the source of capitalism's essential flaw. It begins with the requirement to pay one's debts when due. That is only a requirement when it is systemic, when it is taken to be always in force: the survival constraint.

The question this critique leaves, finally, is this: why do we experience the survival constraint as binding? Financialization carries market logic to ever more extreme heights, but this only makes plain the contradiction that was there in the first place. In this direction I can only point, for now, in the direction of Graeber (2011), who notes the historically exceptional nature of market logic, and of Konings (2015), who asks about its emotional structure. Minsky, writing for a different purpose and audience, was examining an aspect of the same question.

## Disciplinarity and study

The relationship between Minsky's work and the economics discipline might best be characterized as antipathy. Minsky made
clear his disdain for economists' conventions, from the marginal
approach to individual behavior to the dismissal of econometric
results as stale "printouts." Perhaps their greatest sin was that
economic models allowed money only as an artificial construction.
Not only do they take little account of anything like the institutional characteristics of the actual payment system, but money is
dismissed as illusory and thus a distraction from the main event.
That recurrent, costly, and disruptive crisis did not seem to qualify
as counterevidence against these conventions showed that economists placed faith in their discipline above facts and evidence
– though articulating that view hardly helped Minsky win converts.
    Economists, by and large, have responded with similar disdain.
The fact that Minsky did succeed in building an audience meant
that he could not simply be ignored, but still, his rejection of the
mainstream constituted the basis for summary dismissal: "Perhaps
more important than these problems is Minsky's failure to do
justice to those mainstream economists who have emphasized both
finance and stability" (Flemming 1982, 39). It should not be the
cause of much surprise that I am more on the side of Minsky than
of those economists who stand by the discipline's methodological
requirements. My concern here, however, is not with the substance
of the arguments Minsky made to his colleagues, but rather with
the very fact of such arguments.
    There are those heterodox economists, notably the post-
Keynesians, who cite the value of Minsky's insights into the
behavior of capitalism in support of their preferred methodological
conventions. The logic of the heterodox position is that what is
wrong with orthodox economics is the entrenchment of a wrong
theory of the economy in the legitimating institutions of the discipline, in its departments, journals, textbooks, and policy-advising
apparatus; the needed response is then to displace and eventually
overthrow that orthodoxy with what are now outsider positions,
but which can become insider positions. Heterodox economists
celebrate their securing a hold over some share of the departments,
journals, textbooks, and policy-advising apparatus (Lavoie 2006).
    I do not dispute the diagnosis. Minsky is entirely correct when
he says – repeatedly – that a theory of the economy with no role

for financial institutions or anything like money can say little about financial crisis. Orthodox economic theory offered scant guidance before and during 2008, and offers little insight into the crisis in retrospect. (The valuable insights have come from other camps, certainly including heterodox camps (Bezemer 2010).) Yet the orthodoxy remains the core of economics as a subject for research, teaching, and policy-making. This dominance is very much in spite of its limp response to the devastation of the crisis: that failure has proven to be counterbalanced by a disciplinary structure that serves to maintain the status of the orthodoxy by conditioning what research finds publication, what researchers get what jobs, and so on.

But here I part ways with the heterodoxy. Today's outsiders aspire to become tomorrow's insiders; what today is peripheral research, published in marginal journals and codified in marginal textbooks, will tomorrow occupy the core institutions. But how could such a program succeed? Only by establishing new disciplinary norms. Today's outsiders will tomorrow use their insider position to defend their institutional fortifications just as today's insiders do; they will have little choice but to do so, or else what value would there be in taking over journals and departments? The heterodoxy might object with paeans to plurality, but plurality is no way to hold the commanding heights: it is an inherently heterodox stance, and could not survive the ascent to orthodoxy. The only thing worse is to build an intellectual empire based on heterodoxy: it is an investment in outsider status, a sunk cost, and can come only at the cost of keeping others even farther out. The present volume might even be enough to evoke such a response, given the various heterodox claims to Minsky's legacy.

The problem is not the details of the current disciplinary norms of economics; the problem is its definition by disciplinary norms in the first place. An economics that is defined by fealty to methodology, whatever its allegiances, lineage, and political avowals, can only be unscientific. When the choice is between understanding the world and giving up a comfortable and privileged claim to the legitimating mechanisms of such a discipline, any such orthodoxy will face an existential choice, and so will take disciplinarity over study. This is what today's economic orthodoxy has done; an ascendant heterodoxy would do no different.

Minsky, I propose, offers a model for a different economics, a critical economics. Each economist, he said, must "extract meaning from events and institutional changes and integrate the reading of what happened and what is into an interpretation" (1992b, 365). Such is an economics defined by its object – events and institutional changes – not by the form of the interpretation. It is thus not a discipline, structured by exclusions and inclusions and measured by conformance to norms; but rather a set of interpretations, engaging with society, responding to its changes, and structured by the work of interpreters situating themselves in relation to one another, not as insiders and outsiders, but in symmetry.

The economics I am proposing already exists. It is neither orthodox, seeking truth in observance of the law, nor heterodox, seeking truth in transgression of the law. Its only relation to disciplinary norms is to ask what they are for, whose interest they sustain, and thus to challenge them by questioning. Such an economics exists everywhere that economists begin with thoughtful teaching, reading, and writing, and with relentless focus on the texts and institutions that inform them. Minsky's work is a part of this economics: it begins with vision, and bequeaths possibility.

## Minsky's economics

What is Minsky's economics? His work has not found easy categorization – as we have seen, he drew from many teachers, and engaged with many different schools of thought. Minsky rejected with disdain the methodological norms of the academic discipline, and the discipline in turn has largely rejected his challenging body of work. Those heterodox schools that have chosen to count Minsky among their number have not in general accepted the core of his view: an insistence on the foundational status of an understanding of finance that begins from cash flows.

In the preceding chapters, Minsky's body of work served as the scaffolding for an illustration of his way of knowing. Each of his major projects offered new opportunities for study, and the resulting work showed a maintained theory that evolved over time as a result.

Minsky set off from his inspiring Chicago professors, Lange (1981d; 1985b; Lange 1938) and Simons. Lange provided a vision of how market socialism could be made to work; Simons provided a vision of how market capitalism could be made to work. Accepting the conclusions of neither, Minsky took inspiration from both. At Harvard, Schumpeter encouraged him to lead with a vision; Schumpeter's own expansive work provided Minsky not only with an admirable model for inquiry, but also, placing the money markets at the center of capitalism, with a starting point. Minsky's dissertation (1954) established the intellectual mission – to add serious consideration of liquidity to a Schumpeterian sense of business cycles – as well as an operating principle – to put vision first. For Minsky the graduate student, the vision was incipient, sensed but not yet distinguished from the analytical priors of his Harvard training.

The study for the Commission on Money and Credit (1964a) clarified the relationship: his vision was for an entirely new mode of economic analysis. Economists would require convincing, but the study itself was an opportunity to do that, and its expansive scale signaled Minsky's intention to match the opportunity with creative energy. The theoretical work of the dissertation was still present, but the arguments were more confident: Minsky was not responding to his teachers as their student, but reaching out to his colleagues as their peer.

The volume on California banking (1965b; 1965c) stands out among these early works. The state of California was not a natural unit of analysis for Minsky: it lacked the decision-making autonomy of a firm or a household, and though it had a political identity, in monetary and productive terms it was more a constituent region of the US than a unitary entity. This is not to say, of course, that the choice was arbitrary; rather the logic of the choice was in the opportunity for study, created by circumstances. The object of study determined by those circumstances, and the work that came in response, are nonetheless evidently Minsky's: it was an opportunity to confront a maintained theory, the product of study that had come before, with a new set of facts. The work produced a new version of the theory, the basis for study that was still to follow.

New texts affected the maintained theory in much the same way. As the 1965 book marked engagement with California banking, *John Maynard Keynes* (1975c) marked engagement with *The General Theory*. The effort was ambiguous. Minsky presented his work as reclaiming the neglected essential message of Keynes's text, and surely he did identify and develop an important insight from Keynes: the relationship between uncertainty, liquidity, and productive activity. But Minsky's book is just as surely, and perhaps more overtly, an expression of his own insights, not really those of Keynes. Minsky found allies and an audience among the interpreters of Keynes; his central message, however, in the 1975 book as always, was that what was essential was to take explicit account of cash commitments, of the financial structure of capitalism, and this message was largely lost.

Minsky's essays on international money in the late 1970s and early 1980s are a response to the California banking study, integrated now into a more mature theory of capitalism. That theory, as always, took the nation-state as its most natural field of analysis. As the California study had required a narrowed focus to adapt to regional analysis, so the disruptions of the international monetary system required a widened focus to adapt to international analysis. The theory proved flexible: insights about California's integration into the US monetary system were adaptable to the status of the US in the global monetary system. The work of adaptation, as always, left its own trace in Minsky's maintained theory.

*Stabilizing an Unstable Economy* (1986e) was Minsky's last big effort. It can be unsatisfying: Minsky's own frustrations with the state of economic theory, with the economic policy-making informed by that theory, and with the increasingly fragile financial system that seemed to be the result are on full display. His was a theory that offered an explanation of that instability, and the evidence in favor seemed to justify the intellectual energy that would be needed to refound economics. He was sure of his insights, however, and in that way his response was admirable: what was required was to have another go, and so he did. Read as a magnum opus, as the most complete expression of what had come before, the book is satisfyingly intricate as it tries to sort out each issue, major and minor, that had emerged over the decades.

A life's work does not proceed neatly in chapters; these major projects overlapped with many smaller ones. Still, read as one, Minsky's body of work is quite coherent. The chapters of the present book have reflected that coherence in two themes: as a theory of capitalism, and as a way of studying society. The theory of capitalism yields Minsky's most enduring observation: that stability is destabilizing and so instability is inevitable. But it is a theory of capitalism for the stable as well as the unstable moments: to see crisis only as discontinuity is to suppose that it is in some way outside the bounds of study, which would be to excuse capitalism's essential flaw.

Minsky's way of studying society, his way of knowing, is similarly elusive. His was an intellectual life of successive engagement with unfolding contemporaneous history. His ventures in economic theory should likewise be understood as engagements, efforts to interpret and communicate with his colleagues, and not as the outlines of a new economics discipline to be established and defended. Each engagement, whether with text or with event, served as an occasion for study and incremental interpretation. Minsky's approach shows us that the contributions of economists, including his own, should not be evaluated as more or less perfect elaborations of an accepted methodology, or as proposals for what should be the accepted methodology. Instead they should be put to use as the basis for yet more contributions.

The value of such study can be found only in the further study it enables. The work is never done, because its objective is not completion.

# Bibliography

Arrow, Kenneth J., and Frank H. Hahn. 1971. *General Competitive Analysis.* San Francisco: Holden-Day.

Auerback, Marshall, Paul McCulley, and Robert W. Parenteau. 2010. "What Would Minsky Do?" In *The Elgar Companion to Hyman Minsky*, edited by Dimitri B. Papadimitriou and L. Randall Wray. Cheltenham: Edward Elgar.

Bagehot, Walter. 1873. *Lombard Street: A Description of the Money Market.* London: Henry S. King.

Bezemer, Dirk J. 2010. "Understanding Financial Crisis Through Accounting Models." *Accounting, Organizations, and Society* 35 (7): 676–88.

Board of Governors of the Federal Reserve System. 1967. *Fifty-Third Annual Report.* Washington, DC: Board of Governors of the Federal Reserve System.

Brimmer, Andrew F. 1989. "Distinguished Lecture on Economics in Government: Central Banking and Systemic Risks in Capital Markets." *The Journal of Economic Perspectives* 3 (2): 3–16. http://www.jstor.org/stable/1942665?seq=1#page_scan_tab_contents.

Brunnermeier, Markus K., and Lars Heje Pedersen. 2009. "Market Liquidity and Funding Liquidity." *Review of Financial Studies* 22 (6): 2201–38.

Copeland, Morris A. 1952. *A Study of Moneyflows in the United States.* New York: National Bureau of Economic Research.

Delli Gatti, Domenico, and Mauro Gallegati. 1997. "At the Root of the Financial Instability Hypothesis: 'Induced Investment and Business Cycles'." *Journal of Economic Issues* 31 (2): 527–34. http://www.jstor.org/stable/4227204.

Dow, Sheila. 2010. "The Psychology of Financial Markets: Keynes, Minsky, and Emotional Finance." In *The Elgar Companion to Hyman Minsky*, edited by Dimitri B. Papadimitriou and L. Randall Wray. Cheltenham: Edward Elgar.

———. 2012. "Uncertainty-Denial." Discussion Paper DDP1204. University of Victoria Department of Economics.

FCIC (Financial Crisis Inquiry Commission). 2011. *The Financial Crisis Inquiry Report*. New York: PublicAffairs.

Ferri, Piero, and Hyman P. Minsky. 1989. "The Breakdown of the ISLM Synthesis: Implications for Post-Keynesian Economic Theory." *Review of Political Economy* 1: 125–43.

———. 1992. "Market Processes and Thwarting Systems." *Structural Change and Economic Dynamics* 3 (1): 79–91.

Flemming, J. S. 1982. "Comment." In *Financial Crises: Theory, History, and Policy*, edited by Charles P. Kindleberger and Jean-Pierre Laffargue. Cambridge: Cambridge University Press.

Glissant, Édouard. 1997. *Poetics of Relation*. Ann Arbor: University of Michigan Press.

Goodhart, C. A. E. 1984. "Problems of Monetary Management: The UK Experience." In *Monetary Theory and Practice: The UK Experience*. London: Macmillan. doi:10.1007/978-1-349-17295-5_4.

Grad, David, Perry Mehrling, and Daniel H. Neilson. 2011. "Evolution of Last-Resort Operations in the Global Credit Crisis." http://ssrn.com/abstract=2232348.

Graeber, David. 2011. *Debt: The First 5,000 Years*. Brooklyn: Melville House.

Hahn, F. H. 1983. *Money and Inflation*. Cambridge, MA: MIT Press.

Harris, Larry. 2003. *Trading and Exchanges: Market Microstructure for Practitioners*. Oxford: Oxford University Press.

Hawtrey, R. G. 1919. *Currency and Credit*. London: Longmans, Green.

Hicks, John. 1989. *A Market Theory of Money*. Oxford: Oxford University Press.

Hilferding, Rudolf. 1981. *Finance Capital: A Study of the Latest Phase of Capitalist Development*, edited by Tom Bottomore. London: Routledge; Kegan Paul.

hooks, bell. 1994. *Teaching to Transgress: Education as the Practice of Freedom*. New York: Routledge.

Hughes, Jonathan. 1986. *The Vital Few: The Entrepreneur and American Economic Progress*. Oxford: Oxford University Press.

Humphrey, Caroline. 1985. "Barter and Economic Disintegration." *Man* 20 (1): 48–72.

Illich, Ivan. 1976. *Medical Nemesis*. New York: Random House.

Jacotot, Joseph. 1823. *Langue Maternelle*. Louvain: De Pauw.

Jameson, Fredric. 1997. "Culture and Finance Capital." *Critical Inquiry* 24 (1): 246–65.

Kalecki, Michał. 1971. *Selected Essays on the Dynamics of the Capitalist Economy (1933–1970)*. Cambridge: Cambridge University Press.

Keen, Steve. 1995. "Finance and Economic Breakdown: Modeling Minsky's

'Financial Instability Hypothesis'." *Journal of Post Keynesian Economics* 17 (4): 607–35.

——. 2011. *Debunking Economics: The Naked Emperor Dethroned?* Rev. edn. London: Zed Books.

——. 2017. *Can We Avoid Another Financial Crisis?* Cambridge: Polity.

Keynes, John Maynard. 1930. *A Treatise on Money.* London: Macmillan.

——. 1936. *The General Theory of Employment, Interest and Money.* London: Macmillan.

——. 1937. "The General Theory of Employment." *Quarterly Journal of Economics* 51 (2): 209–33.

Kindleberger, Charles P., Emile Despres, and Walter S. Salant. 1966. "The Dollar and World Liquidity: A Minority View." *The Economist* 218 (6389): 526–9.

Knight, Frank. 1921. *Risk, Uncertainty and Profit.* Boston: Houghton Mifflin.

Konings, Martijn. 2015. *The Emotional Logic of Capitalism: What Progressives Have Missed.* Stanford: Stanford University Press.

——. 2018. *Capital and Time: For a New Critique of Neoliberal Reason.* Stanford: Stanford University Press.

Lange, Oskar. 1938. "On the Economic Theory of Socialism." In *On the Economic Theory of Socialism*, edited by Benjamin E. Lippincott. New York: McGraw-Hill.

Lavoie, Marc. 2006. *Introduction to Post-Keynesian Economics.* Basingstoke: Palgrave Macmillan.

——. 2013. "The Monetary and Fiscal Nexus of Neo-Chartalism: A Friendly Critique." *Journal of Economic Issues* 47 (1): 1–32.

McCulley, Paul A. 2001. "Capitalism's Beast of Burden." https://www.pimco.com/en-us/insights/economic-and-market-commentary/global-central-bank-focus/capitalisms-beast-of-burden.

Mehrling, Perry. 1999. "The Vision of Hyman P. Minsky." *Journal of Economic Behavior & Organization* 39 (2): 129–58. http://www.sciencedirect.com/science/article/B6V8F-3WWV211-1/2/dfdaa0f0d703ccd45aa89ab7c5c0712a.

——. 2000. "Minsky and Modern Finance." *Journal of Portfolio Management* 26: 81–8.

——. 2010. *The New Lombard Street: How the Fed Became the Dealer of Last Resort.* Princeton: Princeton University Press.

——. 2017. "Financialization and Its Discontents." *Finance and Society*, early view: 1–10.

Mehrling, Perry, Zoltan Pozsar, James Sweeney, and Daniel H. Neilson. 2013. "Bagehot Was a Shadow Banker: Shadow Banking, Central Banking, and the Future of Global Finance." https://papers.ssrn.com/sol3/papers.cfm?abstract_id=2232016.

Minsky, Hyman P. 1954. "Induced Investment and Business Cycles." PhD thesis, Harvard University. (Published 2000 as *Induced Investment and Business Cycles.* Cheltenham: Edward Elgar.)

——. 1957a. "Central Banking and Money Market Changes." *The Quarterly Journal of Economics* 71 (2): 171–87.

——. 1957b. "Monetary Systems and Accelerator Models." *American Economic Review* 47 (6): 859–83.

——. 1959a. "A Linear Model of Cyclical Growth." *Review of Economics and Statistics* 41 (2): 133–45.

——. 1959b. "Indicators of the Developmental Status of an Economy." *Economic Development and Cultural Change* 7: 151–72.

——. 1959c. "The Effects of Monopolistic and Quasi-Monopolistic Practices on Price Levels." In *Employment, Growth, and Price Levels: Report of the Joint Economic Committee, 86th Congress, 1st Session, Part 7*. Washington, DC: U.S. Government Printing Office.

——. 1961. "Employment Growth and Price Levels: A Review Article." *Review of Economics and Statistics* 43 (1): 1–12.

——. 1962. "Financial Constraints Upon Decisions, an Aggregate View." *Proceedings of the American Statistical Association*: 256–67.

——. 1963a. "Can 'It' Happen Again?" In *Banking and Monetary Studies*. Homewood: Irwin.

——. 1963b. "Financial Institutions and Monetary Policy: Discussion." *American Economic Review* 53 (2): 411–12.

——. 1963c. "Comments on Friedman's and Schwartz' Money and the Business Cycles." *The Review of Economics and Statistics* 45 (1, part 2, Supplement): 64–78.

——. 1964a. "Financial Crisis, Financial Systems, and the Performance of the Economy." In *Private Capital Markets*, 173–380. Englewood Cliffs: Prentice Hall.

——. 1964b. "Longer Waves in Financial Relations: Financial Factors in the More Severe Depressions." *American Economic Review Papers and Proceedings* 54 (3): 324–35.

——. 1965a. "Address Presented at a Conference on 'Labor and the War Against Poverty'." http://digitalassets.lib.berkeley.edu/irle/ucb/text/ir00013.pdf.

——. 1965b. "Commercial Banking and Rapid Economic Growth in California." In *California Banking in a Growing Economy: 1946–1975*, edited by Hyman P. Minsky. Berkeley, CA: Institute of Business and Economic Research.

——. 1965c. "Overview." In *California Banking in a Growing Economy: 1946–1975*, edited by Hyman P. Minsky. Berkeley, CA: Institute of Business and Economic Research.

——. 1965d. "The Integration of Simple Growth and Cycle Models." In *Patterns of Market Behavior: Essays in Honor of Philip Taft*, edited by M. J. Brennan. Providence: Brown University Press.

——. 1965e. "The Role of Employment Policy." In *Poverty in America*, edited by M. Gordon. San Francisco: Chandler.

——. 1966a. "Statement." In *The Federal Reserve Portfolio: Statements by*

*Individual Economists, Joint Economic Committee, 89th Congress, 2nd Session.* Washington, DC: U.S. Government Printing Office.

———. 1966b. "The Evolution of American Banking: The Longer View." *The Bankers' Magazine* 202: 325–9, 397–400.

———. 1966c. "Tight Full Employment: Let's Heat Up the Economy." In *Poverty American Style*, edited by H. Miller. Wadsworth: Belmont.

———. 1967a. "Financial Intermediation in the Money and Capital Markets." In *Issues in Banking and Monetary Analysis*, edited by Giulio Pontecorvo, Robert P. Shay, and Albert G. Hart. New York: Holt, Rinehart, and Winston.

———. 1967b. "Money, Other Financial Variables and Aggregate Demand in the Short Run." In *Monetary Process and Policy: A Symposium*, edited by G. Horwich. Homewood: Irwin.

———. 1968a. "Adequate Aggregate Demand and the Commitment to End Poverty." In *Rural Poverty in the United States: President's National Advisory Commission on Rural Poverty*. Washington, DC:U.S. Government Printing Office.

———. 1968b. "The Crunch and Its Aftermath." *The Bankers' Magazine* 205: 78–82, 171–3.

———. 1968c. "The Crunch of 1966: Model for New Financial Crises?" *Trans-Action* 5 (4): 44–51.

———. 1968d. "Effects of Shifts of Aggregate Demand Upon Income Distribution." *American Journal of Agricultural Economics* 50 (2): 328–39.

———. 1968e. [printed as "Hymen"] "Review of Staffan Burenstam Linder, Trade and Trade Policy for Development." *The Pakistan Development Review* 8 (3): 500–3.

———. 1969a. "Private Sector Asset Management and the Effectiveness of Monetary Policy: Theory and Practice." *Journal of Finance* 24 (2): 223–38.

———. 1969b. "The New Uses of Monetary Powers." *Nebraska Journal of Economics and Business* 8: 3–15.

———. 1969c. "Financial Model Building and Federal Reserve Policy: Discussion." *Journal of Finance* 24 (2): 295–7.

———. 1970a. "How Serious Is the U.S. Recession?" *The Times*, p. 15.

———. 1970b. "Passage to Pakistan." *Trans-Action* 7 (4): 27–39.

———. 1971. "'The Allocation of Social Risk': Discussion." *American Economic Review* 61 (2): 389–90.

———. 1972a. "An Evaluation of Recent Monetary Policy." *Nebraska Journal of Economics and Business* 11 (4): 37–56.

———. 1972b. "An Evaluation of Recent U.S. Monetary Policy." *The Bankers' Magazine* 214: 141–2, 181–5, 229–35.

———. 1972c. "An Exposition of a Keynesian Theory of Investment." In *Mathematical Methods in Investment and Finance*. Amsterdam: Elsevier.

———. 1972d. "Financial Instability Revisited: The Economics of Disaster." In *Reappraisal of the Federal Reserve Discount Mechanism*. St. Louis: Board of Governors, Federal Reserve System.

——. 1973a. "Problems of U.S. Monetary Policy in 1973." *The Bankers' Magazine* 216: 63–8.

——. 1973b. "The Strategy of Economic Policy and Income Distribution." *The Annals of the American Academy of Political and Social Science* 409: 92–101.

——. 1974a. "Can and Should the Fed 'Go It Alone'?" *The Journal of Commerce* 1: 17.

——. 1974b. "Money and the Real World: A Review Article." *Quarterly Review of Economics and Business* 14 (2): 7–17.

——. 1974c. "The Modeling of Financial Instability: An Introduction." In *Modeling and Simulation 5: Proceedings of the Fifth Annual Pittsburgh Conference*. Research Triangle Park, NC: Instrument Society of America.

——. 1974d. "The State of the Economy and of Economics." *Washington University Magazine*, July: 30–4.

——. 1974e. "'Fragile' Financial System Risks Crisis: Deflation; Debt Reduction Essential." *The Money Manager*, August: 7.

——. 1974f. "Review of F. G. Johnson and A. R. Nobay, 'Issues in Monetary Economics'." *The Economic Journal* 84 (336): 996–7.

——. 1975a. "Financial Instability, the Current Dilemma, and the Structure of Banking and Finance." In *Compendium on Major Issues in Bank Regulation: United States Senate, Committee on Banking, Housing, and Urban Affairs, 94th Congress, 1st Session*. Washington, DC: U.S. Government Printing Office.

——. 1975b. "Financial Resources in a Fragile Financial Environment." *Challenge* 18: 6–13.

——. 1975c. *John Maynard Keynes*. New York: Columbia University Press.

——. 1975d. "Suggestions for a Cash-Flow Oriented Bank Examination." In *Proceedings of a Conference on Bank Structure and Competition*. Chicago: Federal Reserve Bank of Chicago.

——. 1976. "Our Financial Heritage and the Prospects of 1976." In *The Outlook for 1976*. Ann Arbor: University of Michigan Annual Conference of the Economic Outlook.

——. 1977a. "An 'Economics of Keynes' Perspective on Money." In *Modern Economic Thought*, edited by S. Weintraub. Philadelphia: University of Pennsylvania Press.

——. 1977b. "A Theory of Systemic Fragility." In *Financial Crises*, edited by E. D. Altman and A. W. Sametz. New York: Wiley Interscience.

——. 1977c. "Banking and a Fragile Financial Environment." *Journal of Portfolio Management* 3 (4): 16–22.

——. 1977d. "How 'Standard' Is Standard Economics?" *Society* 14: 24–9.

——. 1977e. "Statement on the Adequacy of Bank Supervision." In *Committee on Banking, Housing, and Urban Affairs of the United States Senate*. n.p.

——. 1977f. "The Financial Instability Hypothesis: An Interpretation of Keynes and an Alternative to 'Standard' Theory." *Nebraska Journal of Economics and Business* 16 (1): 5–16.

——. 1977g. "The Roots of Current Economic Problems." *Public Interest Economics*, December: 3.

——. 1978a. "Managing Money." In *Special Study on Economic Change: Joint Economic Committee, 75th Congress, 2nd Session*. Washington, DC: U.S. Government Printing Office.

——. 1978b. "The Carter Economics: A Symposium." *Journal of Post-Keynesian Economics* 1 (1): 19–45.

——. 1978c. "The Dollar: U.S. Must Be Seen as an Ailing Bank." *The Money Manager*, April 24, pp. 1–4.

——. 1978d. "The Financial Instability Hypothesis: A Restatement." In *Thames Papers in Political Economy*. London: North East London Polytechnic.

——. 1978e. "U.S. Efforts to Prevent Deep Slump Fan Inflation, Render Policy Helpless." *The Money Manager*, July 10, p. 5.

——. 1978f. "Unless Corrected, Deficit in Trade Could Trigger Bigger Financial Crisis." *The Money Manager*, December 4, pp. 1–4.

——. 1979. "Financial Interrelations, the Balance of Payments and the Dollar Crisis." In *Debt and the Less Developed Countries*, edited by Johnathan D. Aronson. Boulder: Westview Press.

——. 1980a. "Finance and Profits: The Changing Nature of American Business Cycles." In *The Business Cycle and Public Policy 1929–1980: A Compendium of Papers Submitted to the Joint Economic Committee*, edited by 2nd Session 96th Congress. Washington, DC: U.S. Government Printing Office.

——. 1980b. "Money, Financial Markets, and the Coherence of a Market Economy." *Journal of Post Keynesian Economics* 3 (1): 21–31. http://search.ebscohost.com/login.aspx?direct=true&db=bth&AN=8630496&site=ehost-live.

——. 1980c. "The Federal Reserve: Between a Rock and a Hard Place." *Challenge* 23: 30–6.

——. 1980d. "Discussion of the Taylor Paper." *Federal Reserve Bank of St. Louis Review*, April: 113–26.

——. 1980e. "Capitalist Financial Processes and the Instability of Capitalism." *Journal of Economic Issues* 14 (2): 505–22.

——. 1981a. "Finance and Profits: The Pitfalls of Stabilization Policy in Our Economy." In *Perspectives on the Stagflation Economy*. Prepared for the Third Annual Sewanee Economics Symposium.

——. 1981b. "Financial Markets and Economic Instability, 1965–1980." *Nebraska Journal of Economics and Business* 20 (4): 5–16.

——. 1981c. "James Tobin's Asset Accumulation and Economic Activity: A Review Article." *Eastern Economic Journal* 7 (3–4): 199–209.

——. 1981d. "The Breakdown of the 1960s Policy Synthesis." *Telos* 50: 49–58.

——. 1981e. "The United States' Economy in the 1980s: The Financial Past and Present as a Guide to the Future." *Giornale degli Economisti e Annali di Economia* 40 (5–6): 301–17.

——. 1981f. "Review of N. Kaldor: Essays on Economic Stability and Growth." *Journal of Economic Literature* 19 (4): 1574–7.

——. 1982a. "Can 'It' Happen Again? A Reprise." *Challenge* 25 (3): 5–13. http://search.ebscohost.com.monstera.cc.columbia.edu:2048/login.aspx?direct=true&db=eoh&AN=0129398&site=ehost-live.

——. 1982b. *Can "It" Happen Again? Essays on Instability and Finance.* Armonk: M. E. Sharpe.

——. 1982c. "Debt Deflation Processes in Today's Institutional Environment." *Banca Nazionale del Lavoro Quarterly Review* 143: 375–95.

——. 1982d. "The Financial-Instability Hypothesis: Capitalist Processes and the Behavior of the Economy." In *Financial Crises: Theory, History and Policy*, edited by Charles P. Kindleberger and Jean-Pierre Laffargue. Cambridge: Cambridge University Press.

——. 1982e. "Review of Axel Leijonhufvud, 'Information and Coordination'." *The Economic Journal* 91: 976–7.

——. 1983a. "Institutional Roots of American Inflation." In *Inflation Through the Ages: Economic, Social Psychological and Historical Aspects*, edited by Nathan Schmukler and Edward Marcus. New York: Columbia University Press.

——. 1983b. "Notes on Effective Demand." In *Distribution, Effective Demand, and International Economic Relations*, edited by Jan Kregel. London: Macmillan.

——. 1983c. "Pitfalls Due to Financial Fragility." In *Reaganomics in the Stagflation Economy*, edited by Marvin Goodstein and Sidney Weintraub. Philadelphia: University of Pennsylvania Press.

——. 1983d. "Review of Wallace C. Peterson, 'Our Overloaded Economy'." *Journal of Economic Issues* 17: 228–32.

——. 1983e. "The Legacy of Keynes." *Metroeconomica* 35: 87–103.

——. 1984a. "Banking and Industry Between the Two Wars: The United States." *Journal of European Economic History* 13 (2): 235–72.

——. 1984b. "Financial Innovations and Financial Instability: Observations and Theory." In *Financial Innovations: Their Impact on Monetary Policy and Financial Markets.* Boston: Federal Reserve Bank of St. Louis, Kluwer-Nijhoff.

——. 1984c. "Frank Hahn's 'Money and Inflation': A Review Article." *Journal of Post-Keynesian Economics* 3: 449–57.

——. 1984d. "The International Ponzi Scheme." *The Boston Globe*, July 5, op-ed page.

——. 1984e. "The Potential for Financial Crises." In *The Future of the International Monetary System*, edited by Tamir Agmon, Robert G. Hawkins, and Richard M. Levich. Lexington: Lexington Books.

——. 1985a. "An Introduction to Post-Keynesian Economics." *Economic Forum* 15 (2): 1–13.

——. 1985b. "Beginnings." *Banca Nazionale del Lavoro Quarterly Review* 38 (154): 211–21.

——. 1985c. "Money and the Lender of Last Resort." *Challenge* 28 (1): 12–19.

——. 1985d. "Review of Christian Saint-Etienne, 'The Great Depression 1929–1938: Lessons for the 1980s'." *Journal of Economic Literature* 23: 1226–7.

——. 1985e. "Review of Michael J. Piore and Charles F. Sabel, 'The Second Industrial Divide'." *Challenge* 28: 60–4.

——. 1985f. "The Legacy of Keynes." *The Journal of Economic Education* 16 (1): 5–15.

——. 1986a. "Conflict and Interdependence in a Multipolar World." *Studies in Banking and Finance* 4: 3–22.

——. 1986b. "Global Consequences of Financial Deregulation." In *The Marcus Wallenberg Papers on International Finance*. Washington, DC: International Law Institute; School of Foreign Service, Georgetown University.

——. 1986c. "Money and Crisis in Schumpeter and Keynes." In *The Economic Law of Motion of Modern Society: A Marx–Keynes–Schumpeter Centennial*, edited by J. W. Drukker and H. J. Wagener. Cambridge: Cambridge University Press.

——. 1986d. "Review of Lester G. Thurow, 'The Zero Sum Solution: Building a World-Class American Economy'." *Challenge* 29: 60–4.

——. 1986e. *Stabilizing an Unstable Economy*. New Haven; London: Yale University Press. (2nd edn 2008. New York: McGraw-Hill.)

——. 1986f. "The Crisis of 1983 and the Prospects for Advanced Capitalist Economies." In *Marx, Schumpeter, and Keynes: A Centenary Celebration of Dissent*, edited by Suzanne W Helburn and David F. Bramhall. Armonk: M. E. Sharpe.

——. 1986g. "The Evolution of Financial Institutions and the Performance of the Economy." *Journal of Economic Issues* 20 (2): 345–53.

——. 1987a. "Bashing Bigness – but with Blinders: Review of Walter Adams and James W. Birch, 'The Bigness Complex'." *Challenge* 30: 29–31.

——. 1987b. "Pollyanas of Capitalism." *New York Times*, October 22.

——. 1987c. "Review of Forest Capie and Geoffrey Wood, Eds., 'Financial Crises and the World Banking System'." *Journal of Economic Literature* 25: 1341–2.

——. 1987d. "Review of Susan Strange, 'Casino Capitalism'." *Journal of Economic Literature* 25: 1885–5.

——. 1988a. "Back from the Brink." *Challenge* 31 (1): 22–8.

——. 1988b. "Global Debt: Why Is Cooperation so Difficult? Perspective." In *The Political Economy of International Co-Operation*, edited by Paolo Guerrieri and Pier-Carlo Padoan. London: Croom Helm.

——. 1988c. "In a World of Uncertainty." *Against the Current* 14: 42–4.

——. 1988d. "Review of William Greider, 'Secrets of the Temple: How the Federal Reserve Runs the Country'." *Challenge* 31: 58–62.

——. 1989a. "Comments and Discussion on 'Economic Implications of Extraordinary Movements in Stock Prices.'" *Brookings Papers on Economic Activity* (2): 173–82.

——. 1989b. "Financial Crises and the Evolution of Capitalism: The Crash of '87 – What Does It Mean?" In *Capitalist Development and Crisis Theory: Accumulation, Regulation, and Spatial Restructuring*, edited by Mark Gottdeiner and Nicos Komninos. New York: St. Martin's.

——. 1989c. "Financial Structures: Indebtedness and Credit." In *Money, Credit, and Prices in Keynesian Perspective*, edited by Allain Barrere. New York: St. Martin's.

——. 1990a. "Review of Robert Heilbroner and Peter Bernstein, 'The Debt and the Deficit: False Alarms/Real Possibilities'." *Journal of Economic Literature* 28: 1221–2.

——. 1990b. "Schumpeter: Finance and Evolution." In *Evolving Technology and Market Structure: Studies in Schumpeterian Economics*, edited by A. Heertje and M. Perlman. Ann Arbor: University of Michigan Press.

——. 1990c. "Sraffa and Keynes: Effective Demand in the Long Run." In *Essays on Piero Sraffa: Critical Perspectives on the Revival of Classical Theory*, edited by Krishna Bharadwaj and Bertram Schefold. London: Unwin Hyman.

——. 1991a. "Financial Structure and the Performance of the Economy." https://youtu.be/FLi2wdSA66A.

——. 1991b. "The Financial Instability Hypothesis: A Clarification." In *The Risk of Economic Crisis*, edited by Martin Feldstein. Chicago: University of Chicago Press.

——. 1991c. "Financial Crises: Systemic or Idiosyncratic." Working Paper 51. Jerome Levy Economics Institute, Bard College.

——. 1991c. "The Endogeneity of Money." In *Nicholas Kaldor and Mainstream Economics: Confrontation or Convergence?*, edited by E. Nell and W. Semmler, 207–20. New York: St. Martin's.

——. 1992a. "Profits, Deficits and Instability: A Policy Discussion." In *Profits, Deficits and Instability*, edited by Dimitri B. Papadimitriou. London: Macmillan.

——. 1992b. "Taking Schumpeter's Methodology Seriously: Commentary." In *Entrepreneurship, Technological Innovation and Economic Growth: Studies in the Schumpeterian Tradition*, edited by F. M. Scherer and M. Perlman. Ann Arbor: University of Michigan Press.

——. 1993a. "Community Development Banks: An Idea in Search of Substance." *Challenge* 36 (2): 33–41.

——. 1993b. "On the Non-Neutrality of Money." *Federal Reserve Bank of New York Quarterly Review* 2: 77–82.

——. 1993c. "Schumpeter and Finance." In *Market and Institutions in Economic Development: Essays in Honor of Paolo Sylos Lobini*, edited by S. Biasco, A. Roncaglia, and M. Salvati. New York: St. Martin's.

——. 1994. "Financial Instability Hypothesis." In *The Elgar Companion to Radical Political Economy*, edited by P. Arestis and M. Sawyer. Brookfield: Edward Elgar.

——. 1995a. "Financial Factors in the Economics of Capitalism." *Journal of Financial Services Research* 9: 197–208.

———. 1995b. "Longer Waves in Financial Relations: Financial Factors in the More Severe Depressions II." *Journal of Economic Issues* 29 (1): 83–96.

———. 1995c. "The Creation of a Capitalist Financial System." In *The Global Monetary System After the Fall of the Soviet Empire*, edited by M. Szabo-Pelsoczi. Brookfield: Ashgate.

———. 1996. "Uncertainty and the Institutional Structure of Capitalist Economies." *Journal of Economic Issues* 30 (2): 357–68.

Minsky, Hyman P., and Claudia Campbell. 1990. "Getting Off the Back of a Tiger: The Deposit Insurance Crisis in the United States." In *The Future of Financial Systems and Services: Essays in Honor of Jack Revell*, edited by Edward P. M. Gardener. New York: Springer.

Minsky, Hyman P., and Piero Ferri. 1984. "Prices, Employment, and Profits." *Journal of Post-Keynesian Economics* 6 (4): 489–99.

Moten, Fred, and Stefano Harney. 2010. "Debt and Study." *E-Flux Journal* 14: 1–5.

Pistor, Katharina. 2013. "A Legal Theory of Finance." *Journal of Comparative Economics* 41: 315–30.

Rancière, Jacques. 1987. *Le Maître Ignorant*. Paris: Éditions Fayard.

Schumpeter, Joseph A. 1934. *The Theory of Economic Development*. Cambridge, MA: Harvard University Press.

———. 1939. *Business Cycles*. New York; London: McGraw-Hill.

Shackle, George Lennox Sharman. 1972. *Epistemics and Economics: A Critique of Economic Doctrines*. Cambridge: Cambridge University Press.

———. 1988. *Business, Time, and Thought: Selected Papers of G. L. S. Shackle*, edited by Stephen F. Frowen. Basingstoke: Macmillan.

Simons, Henry C. 1948. *Economic Policy for a Free Society*. Chicago: University of Chicago Press.

Thornton, Henry. 1802. *An Enquiry into the Nature and Effects of the Paper Credit of Great Britain*. London: Hatchard.

Treynor, Jack L. 1987. "The Economics of the Dealer Function." *Financial Analysts Journal* 43 (6): 27–34.

Tymoigne, Éric. 2009. *Central Banking, Asset Prices and Financial Fragility*. London: Routledge.

Unger, Irwin. 1974. *The Movement: The American New Left 1959–1973*. New York: Harper & Row.

Wolfson, Martin H. 1986. *Financial Crises: Understanding the Postwar U.S. Experience*. Armonk: M. E. Sharpe.

Wray, L. Randall. 2016. *Why Minsky Matters*. Princeton: Princeton University Press.

Yanoshak, Nancy, ed. 2011. *Educating Outside the Lines: Bard College at Simon's Rock on a "New Pedagogy" for the Twenty-First Century*. New York: Peter Lang.

# Index